The Stratagems

Frontinus

Sextus Julius Frontinus: Stratagems [1]

Book I

Since I alone of those interested in military science have undertaken to reduce its rules to system,2 and since I seem to have fulfilled that purpose, so far as pains on my part could accomplish it, I still feel under obligation, in order to complete the task I have begun, to summarize in convenient sketches the adroit operations of generals, which the Greeks embrace under the one name strategemata. For in this way commanders will be furnished with specimens of wisdom and foresight, which will serve to foster their own power of conceiving and executing like deeds. There will result the added advantage that a general will not fear the issue of his own stratagem, if he compares it with experiments already successfully made.

I neither ignore nor deny the fact that historians have included in the compass of their works this feature also, nor that authors have already recorded in some fashion all famous examples. But I ought, I think, out of consideration for busy men, to have regard to brevity. For it is a tedious business to hunt out separate examples scattered over the vast body of history; and those who have made selections of notable deeds have overwhelmed the reader by the very mass of material. My effort will be devoted to the task of setting forth, as if in response to questions, and as occasion shall demand, the illustration applicable to the case in point. For having examined the categories, I have in advance mapped out my campaign, so to speak, for the presentation of illustrative examples. Moreover, in order that these may be sifted and properly classified according to the variety of subject-matter, I have divided them into three books. In the first are illustrations of stratagems for use before the battle begins; in the second, those that relate to the battle itself and tend to effect the complete subjugation of the enemy; the third contains stratagems connected with sieges and the raising of sieges. Under these successive classes I have grouped the illustrations appropriate to each.

It is not without justice that I shall claim indulgence for this work, and I beg that no one will charge me with negligence, if he finds that I have passed over some illustration. For who could prove equal to the task of examining all the records which have come down to us in both languages! And so I have purposely allowed myself to skip many things. That I have not done this without reason, those will realize who read the books of others treating of the same subjects; but it will be easy for the reader to supply those examples under each category. For since this work, like my preceding ones, has been undertaken for the benefit of others, rather than for the sake of my own renown, I shall feel that I am being aided, rather than criticized, by those who will make additions to it.

If there prove to be any persons who take an interest in these books, let them remember to discriminate between "strategy" and "stratagems," which are by nature extremely similar. For everything achieved by a commander, be it characterized by foresight, advantage, enterprise, or resolution, will belong under the head of "strategy," while those things which fall under some special type of these will be "stratagems." The essential characteristic of the latter, resting, as it does, on skill and cleverness, is effective quite as much when the enemy is to be evaded as when he is to be crushed. Since in this field certain striking results have been produced by speeches, I have set down examples of these also, as well as of deeds.

Types of stratagems for the guidance of a commander in matters to be attended to before battle:
  I. On concealing one's plans.
  II. On finding out the enemy's plans.
  III. On determining the character of the war.
  IV. On leading an army through places infested by the enemy.
  V. On escaping from difficult situations.
  VI. On laying and meeting ambushes while on the march.
  VII. How to conceal the absence of the things we lack, or to supply substitutes for them.

VIII.   On distracting the attention of the enemy.
IX. On quelling a mutiny of soldiers.
X.   How to check an unseasonable demand for battle.
XI. How to arouse an army's enthusiasm for battle.
XII.   On dispelling the fears inspired in soldiers by adverse omens.

I. On Concealing One's Plans

1 Marcus Porcius Cato believed that, when opportunity offered, the Spanish cities which he had subdued would revolt, relying upon the protection of their walls. He therefore wrote to each of the cities, ordering them to destroy their fortifications, and threatening war unless they obeyed forthwith. He ordered these letters to be delivered to all cities on the same day. Each city supposed that it alone had received the commands; had they known that the same orders had been sent to all, they could have joined forces and refused obedience.3

2 Himilco, the Carthaginian general, desiring to land in Sicily by surprise, made no public announcement as to the destination of his voyage, but gave all the captains sealed letters, in which were instructions what port to make, with further directions that no one should read these, unless separated from the flag-ship by a violent storm.4

3 When Gaius Laelius went as envoy to Syphax, he took with him as spies certain tribunes and centurions whom he represented to be slaves and attendants. One of these, Lucius Statorius, who had been rather frequently in the same camp, and whom certain of the enemy seemed to recognize, Laelius caned as a slave, in order to conceal the man's rank.5

4 Tarquin the Proud,6 having decided that the leading citizens of Gabii should be put to death, and not wishing to confide this purpose to anyone, gave no response to the messenger sent to him by his son, but merely cut off the tallest poppy heads with his cane, as he happened to walk about in the garden. The messenger, returning without an answer, reported to the young Tarquin what he had seen his father doing. The son thereupon understood that the same thing was to be done to the prominent citizens of Gabii.7

5 Gaius Caesar, distrusting the loyalty of the Egyptians, and wishing to give the appearance of indifference, indulged in riotous banqueting, while devoting himself to an inspection of the city8 and its defences, pretending to be captivated by the charm of the place and to be succumbing to the customs and life of the Egyptians. Having made ready his reserves while he thus dissembled, he seized Egypt.9

6 When Ventidius was waging war against the Parthian king Pacorus, knowing that a certain Pharnaeus from the province of Cyrrhestica, one of those pretending to be allies, was revealing to the Parthians all the preparations of his own army, he turned the treachery of the barbarian to his own advantage; for he pretended to be afraid that those things would happen which he was particularly desirous should happen, and pretended to desire those things to happen which he really dreaded. And so, fearful that the Parthians would cross the Euphrates before he could be reinforced by the legions which were stationed beyond the Taurus Mountains in Cappadocia, he earnestly endeavoured to make this traitor, according to his usual perfidy, advise the Parthians to lead their army across through Zeugma, where the route is shortest, and where the Euphrates flows in a deep channel; for he declared that, if the Parthians came by that road, he could avail himself of the protection of the hills for eluding their archers; but that he feared disaster if they should advance by the lower road through the open plains.10 Influenced by this information, the barbarians led their army by a circuitous route over the lower road, and spent above forty days in preparing materials and in constructing a bridge11 across the river at a point where the banks were quite widely separated and where the building of the bridge, therefore, involved more work. Ventidius utilized this interval for reuniting his forces, and having assembled these, three days before the Parthians arrived, he opened battle, conquered Pacorus, and killed him.12

7 Mithridates, when he was blockaded by Pompey and planned to retreat the next day, wishing

to conceal his purpose, made foraging expeditions over a wide territory, and even to the valleys adjacent to the enemy. For the purpose of further averting suspicion, he also arranged conferences for a subsequent date with several of his foes; and ordered numerous fires to be lighted throughout the camp. Then, in the second watch, he led out his forces directly past the camp of the enemy.13

8 When the Emperor Caesar Domitianus Augustus Germanicus wished to crush the Germans, who were in arms, realizing that they would make greater preparations for war if they foresaw the arrival of so eminent a commander as himself, he concealed the reason for his departure from Rome under the pretext of taking a census of the Gallic provinces. Under cover of this he plunged into sudden warfare, crushed the ferocity of these savage tribes, and thus acted for the good of the provinces.14

9 When it was essential that Hasdrubal and his troops should be destroyed before they joined Hannibal, the brother of Hasdrubal, Claudius Nero, lacking confidence in the troops under his own command, was therefore eager to unite his forces with those of his colleague, Livius Salinator, to whom the direction of the campaign had been committed. Desiring, however, that his departure should be unobserved by Hannibal, whose camp was opposite his, he chose ten thousand of his bravest soldiers, and gave orders to the lieutenants whom he left that the usual number of patrols and sentries be posted, the same number of fires lighted, and the usual appearance of the camp be maintained, in order that Hannibal might not become suspicious and venture to attack the few troops left behind. Then, when he joined his colleague in Umbria after secret marches, he forbade the enlargement of the camp, lest he give some sign of his arrival to the Carthaginian commander, who would be likely to refuse battle if he knew the forces of the consuls had been united. Accordingly, attacking the enemy unawares with his reinforced troops, he won the day and returned to Hannibal in advance of any news of his exploit. Thus by the same plan he stole a march on one of the two shrewdest Carthaginian generals and crushed the other.15

10 Themistocles, urging upon his fellow-citizens the speedy construction of the walls which, at the command of the Lacedaemonians, they had demolished, informed the envoys sent from Sparta to remonstrate about this matter, that he himself would come, to put an end to this suspicion. Accordingly he came to Sparta. There, by feigning illness, he secured a considerable delay. But after he realized that his subterfuge was suspected, he declared that the rumour which had come to the Spartans was false, and asked them to send some of their leading men, whose word they would take about the building operations of the Athenians. Then he wrote secretly to the Athenians, telling them to detain those who had come to them, until, upon the restoration of the walls, he could admit to the Spartans that Athens was fortified, and could inform them that their leaders could not return until he himself had been sent back. These terms the Spartans readily fulfilled, that they might not atone for the death of one by that of many.16

11 Lucius Furius, having led his army into an unfavourable position, determined to conceal his anxiety, lest the others take alarm. By gradually changing his course, as though planning to attack the enemy after a wider circuit, he finally reversed his line of march, and led his army safely back, without its knowing what was going on.

12 When Metellus Pius was in Spain and was asked what he was going to do the next day, he replied: "If my tunic could tell, I would burn it."17

13 When Marcus Licinius Crassus was asked at what time he was going to break camp, he replied: "Are you afraid you'll not hear the trumpet?"18

II. On Finding Out the Enemy's Plans

1 Scipio Africanus, seizing the opportunity of sending an embassy to Syphax, commanded specially chosen tribunes and centurions to go with Laelius, disguised as slaves and entrusted with the task of spying out the strength of the king. These men, in order to examine more freely the situation of the camp, purposely let loose a horse and chased it around the greatest

part of the fortifications, pretending it was running away. After they had reported the results of their observations, the destruction of the camp by fire19 brought the war to a close.20

2 During the war with Etruria, when shrewd methods of reconnoitering were still unknown to Roman leaders, Quintus Fabius Maximus commanded his brother, Fabius Caeso, who spoke the Etruscan language fluently, to put on Etruscan dress and to penetrate into the Ciminian Forest, where our soldiers had never before ventured. He showed such discretion and energy in executing these commands, that after traversing the forest and observing that the Umbrians of Camerium were not hostile to the Romans, he brought them into an alliance.21

3 When the Carthaginians saw that the power of Alexander was so great that it menaced even Africa, they ordered one of their citizens, a resolute man named Hamilcar Rhodinus, to go to the king, pretending to be an exile, and to make every effort to gain his friendship. When Rhodinus had succeeded in this, he disclosed to his fellow-citizens the king's plans.22

4 The same Carthaginian sent men to tarry a long time at Rome, in the rôle of ambassadors, and thus to secure information of our plans.

5 When Marcus Cato was in Spain, being unable otherwise to arrive at a knowledge of the enemy's plans, he ordered three hundred soldiers to make a simultaneous attack on an enemy post, to seize one of their men, and to bring him unharmed to camp. The prisoner, under torture, revealed all the secrets of his side.23

6 During the war with the Cimbrians and Teutons, the consul Gaius Marius, wishing to test the loyalty of the Gauls and Ligurians, sent them a letter, commanding them in the first part of the letter not to open the inner part,24 which was specially sealed, before a certain date. Afterwards, before the appointed time had arrived, he demanded the same letter back, and finding all seals broken, he knew that acts of hostility were afoot.25

[There is also another method of securing intelligence, by which the generals themselves, without calling in any outside help, by their own unaided efforts take precautions, as, for instance:]

7 In the Etruscan war, the consul Aemilius Paulus was on the point of sending his army down into the plain near the town of Vetulonia, when he saw afar off a flock of birds rise in somewhat startled flight from a forest, and realized that some treachery was lurking there, both because the birds had risen in alarm and at the same time in great numbers. He therefore sent some scouts ahead and discovered that ten thousand Boii were lying in wait at that point to meet the Roman army. These he overwhelmed by sending his legions against them at a different point from that at which they were expected.26

8 In like manner, Tisamenus, the son of Orestes, hearing that a ridge, a natural stronghold, was held by the enemy, sent men ahead to ascertain the facts; and upon their reporting that his impression was without foundation, he began his march. But when he saw a large number of birds all at once fly from the suspected ridge and not settle down at all, he came to the conclusion that the enemy's troops were hiding there; and so, leading his army by a detour, he escaped those lying in wait for him.27

9 Hasdrubal, brother of Hannibal, knew that the armies of Livius and Nero had united (although by avoiding two separate camps they strove to conceal this fact), because he observed horses rather lean from travel and men somewhat sunburned, as naturally results from marching.28

On Determining the Character of the War

1 Whenever Alexander of Macedon had a strong army, he chose the sort of warfare in which he could fight in open battle.

2 Gaius Caesar, in the Civil War, having an army of veterans and knowing that the enemy had only raw recruits, always strove to fight in open battle.

3 Fabius Maximus, when engaged in war with Hannibal, who was inflated by his success in battle, decided to avoid any dangerous hazards and to devote himself solely to the protection of Italy. By this policy he earned the name of Cunctator ("The Delayer") and the reputation of a consummate general.29

4 The Byzantines in their war with Philip, avoiding all risks of battle, and abandoning even the defence of their territory, retired within the walls of their city and succeeded in causing Philip to withdraw, since he could not endure the delay of a siege.30

5 Hasdrubal, the son of Gisco, in the Second Punic War, distributed his vanquished army among the cities of Spain when Publius Scipio pressed hard upon him. As a result, Scipio, in order not to scatter his forces by laying siege to several towns, withdrew his army into winter quarters.31

6 Themistocles, when Xerxes was approaching, thinking the strength of the Athenians unequal to a land battle, to the defence of their territory, or to the support of a siege, advised them to remove their wives and children to Troezen and other towns, to abandon the city, and to transfer the scene of the war to the water.32

7 Pericles did the same thing in the same state, in the war with the Spartans.33

8 While Hannibal was lingering in Italy, Scipio sent an army into Africa, and so forced the Carthaginians to recall Hannibal. In this way he transferred the war from his own country to that of the enemy.34

9 When the Spartans had fortified Decelea, a stronghold of the Athenians, and were making frequent raids there, the Athenians sent a fleet to harass the Peloponnesus, and thus secured the recall of the army of Spartans stationed at Decelea.35

10 When the Germans, in accordance with their usual custom, kept emerging from woodland-pastures and unsuspected hiding-places to attack our men, and then finding a safe refuge in the depths of the forest, the Emperor Caesar Domitianus Augustus, by advancing the frontier of the empire along a stretch of •one hundred and twenty miles, not only changed the nature of the war, but brought his enemies beneath his sway, by uncovering their hiding-places.36

IV. On Leading an Army through Places Infested by the Enemy

1 When the consul Aemilius Paulus was leading his army along a narrow road near the coast in Lucania, and the fleet of the Tarentines, lying in wait for him, had attacked his troops by means of scorpions,37 he placed prisoners as a screen to his line of march. Not wishing to harm these, the enemy ceased their attacks.38

2 Agesilaus, the Spartan, when returning from Phrygia laden with booty, was hard pressed by the enemy, who took advantage of their position to harass his line of march. He therefore placed a file of captives on each flank of his army. Since these were spared by the enemy, the Spartans found time to pass.39

3 The same Agesilaus, when the Thebans held a pass through which he had to march, turned his course, as if he were hastening to Thebes. Then, when the Thebans withdrew in alarm to protect their walls, Agesilaus resumed his march and arrived at his goal without opposition.40

4 When Nicostratus, king of the Aetolians, was at war with the Epirotes, and could enter their territory only by narrow defiles, he appeared at one point, as if intending to break through at that place. Then, when the whole body of Epirotes rushed thither to prevent this, he left a few of his men to produce the impression that his army was still there, while he himself, with the rest of his troops, entered at another place, where he was not expected.

5 Autophradates, the Persian, upon leading his army into Pisidia, and finding certain passes occupied by the Pisidians, pretended to be thwarted in his plan for crossing, and began to retreat. When the Pisidians were convinced of this, under cover of night he sent a very strong force ahead to seize the same place, and on the following day sent his whole army across.41

6 When Philip of Macedon was aiming at the conquest of Greece, he heard that the Pass of Thermopylae was occupied by Greek troops. Accordingly, when envoys of the Aetolians came to sue for peace, he detained them, while he himself hastened by forced marches to the Pass, and since the guards had relaxed their vigilance while awaiting the return of the envoys, by his unexpected coming he succeeded in marching through the Pass.42

7 When the Athenian general Iphicrates was engaged in a campaign against the Spartan Anaxibius on the Hellespont near Abydus, he had to lead his army on one occasion through

places occupied by enemy patrols, hemmed in on the one side by precipitous mountains, and on the other washed by the sea. For some time he delayed, and then on an unusually cold day, when no one suspected such a move, he selected his most rugged men, rubbed them down with oil and warmed them up with wine, and then ordered them to skirt the very edge of the sea, swimming across the places that were too precipitous to pass. Thus by an unexpected attack from the rear he overwhelmed the guards of the defile.43

8 When Gnaeus Pompey on one occasion was prevented from crossing a river because the enemy's troops were stationed on the opposite bank, he adopted the device of repeatedly leading his troops out of camp and back again. Then, when the enemy were at last tricked into relaxing their watch on the roads in front of the Roman advance, he made a sudden dash and effected a crossing.44

9 When Porus, a king of the Indians, was keeping Alexander of Macedon from leading his troops across the river Hydaspes, the latter commanded his men to make a practice of running toward the water. When by that sort of manoeuvre he had led Porus to guard the opposite bank, he suddenly led his army across at a higher point of the stream.45

9a The same Alexander, prevented by the enemy from crossing the river Indus, began to send horsemen into the water at different points and to threaten to effect a crossing. Then, when he had the barbarians keyed up with expectation, he seized an island a little further off, and from there sent troops to the further bank. When the entire force of the enemy rushed away to overwhelm this band, he himself crossed safely by fords left unguarded and reunited all his troops.45

10 Xenophon once ordered his men to attempt a crossing in two places, in the face of Armenians who had possession of the opposite bank. Being repulsed at the lower point, he passed to the upper; and when driven back from there also by the enemy's attack, he returned to the lower crossing, but only after ordering a part of his soldiers to remain behind and to cross by the upper passage, so soon as the Armenians should return to protect the lower. The Armenians, supposing that all were proceeding to the lower point, overlooked those remaining above, who, crossing the upper ford without molestation, defended their comrades as they also passed over.46

11 When Appius Claudius, consul in the first Punic War, was unable to transport his soldiers from the neighbourhood of Regium to Messina, because the Carthaginians were guarding the Straits, he caused the rumour to be spread that he could not continue a war which had been undertaken without the endorsement of the people, and turning about he pretended to set sail for Italy. Then, when the Carthaginians dispersed, believing he had gone, Appius turned back and landed in Sicily.47

12 When certain Spartan generals had planned to sail to Syracuse, but were afraid of the Carthaginian fleet anchored along the shore, they commanded that the ten Carthaginian ships which they had captured should go ahead as though victors, with their own vessels either lashed to their side or towed behind. Having deceived the Carthaginians by these appearances, the Spartans succeeded in passing by.48

13 When Philip was unable to sail through the straits called Stena,49 because the Athenian fleet kept guard at a strategic point, he wrote to Antipater that Thrace was in revolt, and that the garrisons which he had left there had been cut off, directing Antipater to leave all other matters and follow him. This letter Philip arranged to have fall into the hands of the enemy. The Athenians, imagining they had secured secret intelligence of the Macedonians, withdrew their fleet, while Philip now passed through the straits with no one to hinder him.50

9a The Chersonese happened at one time to be controlled by the Athenians, and Philip was prevented from capturing it, owing to the fact that the strait was commanded by vessels not only of the Byzantines but also of the Rhodians and Chians; but Philip won the confidence of these peoples by returning their captured ships, as pledges of the peace to be arranged between himself and the Byzantines, who were the cause of the war. While the negotiations dragged on for some time and Philip purposely kept changing the details of the terms, in the interval he got ready a fleet, and eluding the enemy while they were off their guard, he suddenly sailed into the straits.51

14 When Chabrias, the Athenian, was unable to secure access to the harbour of the Samians on account of the enemy blockade, he sent a few of his own ships with orders to cross the mouth of the harbour, thinking that the enemy on guard would give chase. When the enemy were drawn away by this ruse, and no one now hindered, he secured possession of the harbour with the remainder of his fleet.52

V. On Escaping from Difficult Situations

1 When Quintus Sertorius, in the Spanish campaign, desired to cross a river while the enemy were harassing him from the rear, he had his men construct p37a crescent-shaped rampart on the bank, pile it high with timber, and set fire to it. When the enemy were thus cut off, he crossed the stream without hindrance.53

2 In like manner Pelopidas, the Theban, in the Thessalian war, sought to cross a certain stream. Choosing a site above the bank larger than was necessary for his camp, he constructed a rampart of chevaux-de-frise and other materials, and set fire to it. Then, while the enemy were kept off by the fire, he crossed the stream.54

3 When Quintus Lutatius Catulus had been repulsed by the Cimbrians, and his only hope of safety lay in passing a stream the banks of which were held by the enemy, he displayed his troops on the nearest mountain, as though intending to camp there. Then he commanded his men not to loose their packs, or put down their loads, and not to quit the ranks or standards. In order the more effectively to strengthen the impression made upon the enemy, he ordered a few tents to be erected in open view, and fires to be built, while some built a rampart and others went forth in plain sight to collect wood. The Cimbrians, deeming these performances genuine, themselves also chose a place for a camp, scattering through the nearest fields to gather the supplies necessary for their stay. In this way they afforded Catulus opportunity not merely to cross the stream, but also to attack their camp.55

4 When Croesus could not ford the Halys, and had neither boats nor the means of building a bridge, he began up stream and constructed a ditch behind his camp, thus bringing the channel of the river in the rear of his army.56

p39 5 When Gnaeus Pompey at Brundisium had planned to leave Italy and to transfer the war to another field, since Caesar was heavy on his heels, just as he was on the point of embarking, he placed obstacles in some roads; others he blocked by constructing walls across them; others he intersected with trenches, setting sharp stakes in the latter, and laying hurdles covered with earth across the openings. Some of the roads leading to the harbour he guarded by throwing beams across and piling them one upon another in a huge heap. After consummating these arrangements, wishing to produce the appearance of intending to retain possession of the city, he left a few archers as a guard on the walls; the remainder of his troops he led out in good order to the ships. Then, when he was under way, the archers also withdrew by familiar roads, and overtook him in small boats.57

6 When the consul Gaius Duellius was caught by a chain stretched across the entrance to the harbour of Syracuse, which he had rashly entered, he assembled all his soldiers in the sterns of the boats, and when the boats were thus tilted up, he propelled them forward with the full force of his oarsmen. Thus lifted up over the chain, the prows moved forward. When this part of the boats had been carried over, the soldiers, returning to the prows, depressed these, and the weight thus transferred to them permitted the boats to pass over the chain.58

7 When Lysander, the Spartan, was blockaded in the harbour59 of the Athenians with his entire fleet, since the ships of the enemy were sunk at the point where the sea flows in through a very narrow entrance, he commanded his men to disembark secretly. Then, placing his ships on wheels, he transported them to the neighbouring harbour of Munychia.60

8 When Hirtuleius, lieutenant of Quintus Sertorius, was leading a few cohorts up a long narrow road in Spain between two precipitous mountains, and had learned that a large

detachment of the enemy was approaching, he had a ditch dug across between the mountains, fenced it with a wooden rampart, set fire to this, and made his escape, while the enemy were thus cut off from attacking him.61

9 When Gaius Caesar led out his forces against Afranius in the Civil War, and had no means of retreating without danger, he had the first and second lines of battle remain in arms, just as they were drawn up, while the third secretly applied itself to work in the rear, and dug a ditch fifteen feet deep, within the line of which the soldiers under arms withdrew at sunset.62

10 Pericles the Athenian, being driven by the Peloponnesians into a place surrounded on all sides by precipitous cliffs and provided with only two outlets, dug a ditch of great breadth on one side, as if to shut out the enemy; on the other side he began to build a road, as if intending to make a sally by this. The besiegers, not supposing that Pericles' army would make its escape by the ditch which he had constructed, massed to oppose him on the side where the road was. But Pericles, spanning the ditch by bridges which he had made ready, extricated his men without interference.63

11 Lysimachus, one of the heirs to Alexander's power, having determined on one occasion to pitch his camp on a high hill, was conducted by the inadvertence of his men to a lower one. Fearing that the enemy would attack from above, he dug a triple line of trenches and encircled these with a rampart. Then, running a single trench around all the tents, he thus fortified the entire camp. Having thus shut off the advance of the enemy, he filled in the ditches with earth and leaves, and made his way across them to higher ground.64

12 Gaius Fonteius Crassus, when in Spain, having set out with three thousand men on a foraging expedition, was caught in an awkward position by Hasdrubal. At nightfall, when such a movement was least expected, communicating his plan only to the centurions of the first rank, he burst through the enemy's patrols.

13 Lucius Furius, having led his army into an unfavourable position, determined to conceal his anxiety, lest the others take alarm. By gradually changing his course, as though planning to attack the enemy after a wider circuit, he finally reversed his line of march, and led his army safely back, without their knowing what was going on.

14 When the consul Cornelius Cossus had been caught in a disadvantageous position by the enemy in the Samnite War, Publius Decius, tribune of the soldiers, urged him to send a small force to occupy a hill near by, and volunteered as leader of those who should be sent. The enemy, thus diverted to a different quarter, allowed the consul to escape, but surrounded Decius and besieged him. But Decius, extricating himself from this predicament by making a sortie at night, escaped with his men unharmed, and rejoined the consul.65

15 Under the consul Atilius Calatinus the same thing was done by a man whose name is variously reported. Some say he was called Laberius, and some Quintus Caedicius, but most give it as Calpurnius Flamma. This man, seeing that the army had entered a valley, the sides and all commanding parts of which the enemy had occupied, asked and received from the consul three hundred soldiers. After exhorting these to save the army by their valour, he hastened to the centre of the valley. To crush him and his followers, the enemy descended from all quarters, but, being held in check in a long and fierce battle, they thus afforded the consul an opportunity to extricate his army.66

16 When the army of the consul Quintus Minucius had marched down into a defile of Liguria, and the memory of the disaster of the Caudine Forks occurred to the minds of all, Minucius ordered the Numidian auxiliaries, who seemed of small account because of their own wild appearance and the ungainliness of their steeds, to ride up to the mouth of the defile which the enemy held. The enemy were at first on the alert against attack, and threw out patrols. But when the Numidians, in order to inspire still more contempt for themselves, purposely affected to fall from their horses and to engage in ridiculous antics, the barbarians, breaking ranks at the novel sight, gave themselves up completely to the enjoyment of the show. When the Numidians noticed this, they gradually grew nearer, and putting spurs to their horses, dashed through the lightly held line of the enemy. Then they set fire to the fields near by, so that it

became necessary for the Ligurians to withdraw to defend their own territory, thereby releasing the Romans shut up at the pass.67

17 In the Social War, Lucius Sulla, surprised in a defile near Aesernia by the army of the enemy under the command of Duillius, asked for a conference, but was unsuccessful in negotiating terms of peace. Noting, however, that the enemy were careless and off their guard as a result of the truce, he marched forth at night, leaving only a trumpeter, with instructions to create the impression of the army's presence by sounding the watches, and to rejoin him when the fourth watch began. In this way he conducted his troops unharmed to a place of safety, with all their baggage and engines of war.68

18 The same Sulla, when fighting in Cappadocia against Archelaus, general of Mithridates, embarrassed by the difficulties of the terrain and the large numbers of the enemy, proposed peace. Then, taking advantage of the opportunity afforded by the truce, which served to divert the watchfulness of his adversary, he slipped out of his hands.69

19 Hasdrubal, brother of Hannibal, when unable to make his way out of a defile the entrance of which was held by the enemy, entered into negotiations with Claudius Nero and promised to withdraw from Spain if allowed to depart. Then, by quibbling over the terms, he dragged out negotiations for several days, during all of which time he was busy sending out his troops in detachments by way of paths so narrow that they were overlooked by the Romans. Finally he himself easily made his escape with the remainder, who were light-armed.70

20 When Marcus Crassus had constructed a ditch around the forces of Spartacus, the latter at night filled it with the bodies of prisoners and cattle that he had slain, and thus marched across it.71

21 The same Spartacus, when besieged on the slopes of Vesuvius at the point where the mountain was steepest and on that account unguarded, plaited ropes of osiers from the woods. Letting himself down by these, he not only made his escape, but by appearing in another quarter struck such terror into Clodius that several cohorts gave way before a force of only seventy-four gladiators.72

22 This Spartacus, when enveloped by the troops of the proconsul Publius Varinius, placed stakes at short intervals before the gate of the camp; then setting up corpses, dressed in clothes and furnished with weapons, he tied these to the stakes to give the appearance of sentries when viewed from a distance. He also lighted fires throughout the whole camp. Deceiving the enemy by this empty show, Spartacus by night silently led out his troops.73

23 When Brasidas, a general of the Spartans, was surprised near Amphipolis by a host of Athenians who outnumbered him, he allowed himself to be enveloped, in order to diminish the density of the enemy's ranks by lengthening the line of besiegers. Then he broke through at the point where the line was most lightly held.74

24 Iphicrates, when campaigning in Thrace, having on one occasion pitched his camp on low ground, discovered through scouts that the neighbouring hill was held by the enemy, and that from it came down a single road which might be utilized to overwhelm him and his men. Accordingly he left a few men in camp at night, and commanded them to light a number of fires. Then leading forth his troops and ranging them along the sides of the road just mentioned, he suffered the barbarians to pass by. When in this way the disadvantage of terrain from which he himself suffered had been turned against them, with part of his army he overwhelmed their rear, while with another part he captured their camp.75

25 Darius, in order to deceive the Scythians, left dogs and asses in camp at his departure. When the enemy heard these barking and braying, they imagined that Darius was still there.76

26 To produce a like misconception in the minds of our men, the Ligurians, in various places, tied bullocks to trees with halters. The animals, being thus separated, bellowed incessantly and produced the impression that the Ligurians were still there.

27 Hanno, when enveloped by the enemy, selected the point in the line best suited for a sortie, and, piling up light stuff, set fire to it. Then, when the enemy withdrew to guard the other exits, he marched his men straight through the fire, directing them to protect their faces with

their shields, and their legs with their clothing.
28 Hannibal on one occasion was embarrassed by difficulties of terrain, by lack of supplies, and by the circumstance that Fabius Maximus was heavy on his heels. Accordingly he tied bundles of lighted fagots to the horns of oxen, and turned the animals loose at night. When the flames spread, fanned by the motion, the panic-stricken oxen ran wildly hither and thither over the mountains to which they had been driven, illuminating the whole scene. The Romans, who had gathered to witness the sight, at first thought a prodigy had occurred. Then, when scouts reported the facts, Fabius, fearing an ambush, kept his men in camp. Meanwhile the barbarians marched away, as no one prevented them.77

VI. On Laying and Meeting Ambushes while on the March

1 When Fulvius Nobilior was leading his army from Samnium against the Lucanians, and had learned from deserters that the enemy intended to attack his rearguard, he ordered his bravest legion to go in advance, and the baggage train to follow in the rear. The enemy, regarding this circumstance as a favourable opportunity, began to plunder the baggage. Fulvius then marshalled five cohorts of the legion I have mentioned above on the right side of the road, and five on the left. Then, when the enemy were intent on plundering, Fulvius, deploying his troops on both flanks, enveloped the foe and cut them to pieces.
2 The same Nobilior on one occasion was hard pressed from the rear by the enemy, as he was on the march. Across his route ran a stream, not so large as to prevent passage, but large enough to cause delay by the swiftness of the current.78 On the nearer side of this, Nobilior placed one legion in hiding, in order that the enemy, despising his small numbers, might follow more boldly. When this expectation was realized, the legion which had been posted for the purpose attacked the enemy from ambush and destroyed them.
3 When Iphicrates was leading his army in Thrace in a long file on account of the nature of the terrain, and the report was brought to him that the enemy planned to attack his rearguard, he ordered some cohorts to withdraw to both flanks and halt, while the rest were to quicken their pace and flee.79 But from the complete line as it passed by, he kept back all the choicest soldiers. Thus, when the enemy were busy with promiscuous pillaging, and in fact were already exhausted, while his own men were refreshed and drawn up in order, he attacked and routed the foe and stripped them of their booty.80
4 When our army was about to pass through the Litana Forest, the Boii cut into the trees at the base, leaving them only a slender support by which to stand, until they should be pushed over. Then the Boii hid at the further edge of the woods and by toppling over the nearest trees caused the fall of those more distant, as soon as our men entered the forest. In that way they spread general disaster among the Romans, and destroyed a large force.81

VII. How to Conceal the Absence of the Things we lack, or to supply Substitutes for Them

1 Lucius Caecilius Metellus, lacking ships with which to transport his elephants, fastened together large earthen jars, covered them with planking, and then, loading the elephants on these, ferried them across the Sicilian Straits.82
2 When Hannibal on one occasion could not force his elephants to ford an especially deep stream, having neither boats nor material of which to construct them, he ordered one of his men to wound the most savage elephant under the ear, and then straightway to swim across the stream and take to his heels. The infuriated elephant, eager to pursue the author of his suffering, swam the stream, and thus set an example for the rest to make the same venture.83
3 When the Carthaginian admirals were about to equip their fleet, but lacked broom,84 they cut off the hair of their women and employed it for making cordage.85
4 The Massilians and Rhodians did the same.
5 Marcus Antonius, when a refugee from Mutina, gave his soldiers bark to use as shields.86

6 Spartacus and his troops had shields made of osiers and covered with hides.87
7 This place, I think, is not inappropriate for recounting that famous deed of Alexander of Macedon. Marching along the desert roads of Africa, and suffering in common with his men from most distressing thirst, when some water was brought him in a helmet by a soldier, he poured it out upon the ground in the sight of all, in this way serving his soldiers better by his example of restraint than if he had been able to share the water with the rest.88

VIII. On Distracting the Attention of the Enemy

1 When Coriolanus was seeking to avenge by war the shame of his own condemnation, he prevented the ravaging of the lands of the patricians, while burning and harrying those of the plebeians, in order to arouse discord whereby to destroy the harmony of the Romans.89
2 When Hannibal had proved no match for Fabius either in character or in generalship, in order to smirch him with dishonour, he spared his lands, when he ravaged all others. To meet this assault, Fabius transferred the title to his property to the State, thus, by his loftiness of character, preventing his honour from falling under the suspicion of his fellow-citizens.90
3 In the fifth consulship of Fabius Maximus, the Gauls, Umbrians, Etruscans, and Samnites had formed an alliance against the Roman people. Against these tribes Fabius first constructed a fortified camp beyond the Apennines in the region of Sentinum. Then he wrote to Fulvius and Postumius, who were guarding the City, directing them to move on Clusium with their forces. When these commanders complied, the Etruscans and Umbrians withdrew to defend their own possessions, while Fabius and his colleague Decius attacked and defeated the remaining forces of Samnites and Gauls.91
4 When the Sabines levied a large army, left their own territory, and invaded ours, Manius Curius by secret routes sent against them a force which ravaged their lands and villages and set fire to them in divers places. In order to avert this destruction of their country, the Sabines thereupon withdrew. But Curius succeeded in devastating their country while it was unguarded, in repelling their army without an engagement, and then in slaughtering it piecemeal.92
5 Titus Didius at one time lacked confidence because of the small number of his troops, but continued the war in hope of the arrival of certain legions which he was awaiting. On hearing that the enemy planned to attack these legions, he called an assembly of the soldiers and ordered them to get ready for battle, and purposely to exercise a careless supervision over their prisoners. As a result, a few of the latter escaped and reported to their people that battle was imminent. The enemy, to avoid dividing their strength when expecting battle, abandoned their plan of attacking those for whom they were lying in wait, so that the legions arrived without hindrance and in perfect safety at the camp of Didius.93
6 In the Punic War certain cities had resolved to revolt from the Romans to the Carthaginians, but wishing, before they revolted, to recover the hostages they had given, they pretended that an uprising had broken out among their neighbours which Roman commissioners ought to come and suppress. When the Romans sent these envoys, the cities detained them as counter-pledges, and refused to restore them until they themselves recovered their own hostages.
7 After defeat of the Carthaginians, King Antiochus sheltered Hannibal and utilized his counsel against the Romans. When Roman envoys were sent to Antiochus, they held frequent conferences with Hannibal, and thus caused him to become an object of suspicion to the king, to whom he was otherwise most agreeable and useful, in consequence of his cleverness and experience in war.94
8 When Quintus Metellus was waging war against Jugurtha, he bribed the envoys sent him to betray the king into his hands. When other envoys came, he did the same; and with a third embassy he adopted the same policy. But his efforts to take Jugurtha prisoner met with small success, for Metellus wished the king to be delivered into his hands alive. And yet he accomplished a great deal, for when his letters addressed to the friends of the king were intercepted, the king punished all these men, and, being thus deprived of advisers, was unable

to secure any friends for the future.95

9 Gaius Caesar on one occasion caught a soldier who had gone to procure water, and learned from him that Afranius and Petreius planned to break camp that night. In order to hamper the plans of the enemy, and yet not cause alarm to his own troops, Caesar early in the evening gave orders to sound the signal for breaking camp, and commanded mules to be driven past the camp of the enemy with noise and shouting. Thinking that Caesar was breaking camp, his adversaries stayed where they were, precisely as Caesar desired.96

10 When, on one occasion, reinforcements and provisions were on the way to Hannibal, Scipio, wishing to intercept these, sent ahead Minucius Thermus, and arranged to come himself to lend his support.97

11 When the Africans were planning to cross over to Sicily in vast numbers in order to attack Dionysius, tyrant of Syracuse, the latter constructed strongholds in many places and commanded their defenders to surrender them at the coming of the enemy, and then, when they retired, to return secretly to Syracuse. The Africans were forced to occupy the captured strongholds with garrisons, whereupon Dionysius, having reduced the army of his opponents to the scanty number which he desired, and being now approximately on an equality, attacked and defeated them, since he had concentrated his own forces, and had separated those of his adversaries.98

12 When Agesilaus, the Spartan, was waging war against Tissaphernes, he pretended to make for Caria, as though likely to fight more advantageously in mountainous districts against an enemy strong in cavalry. When he had advertised to this purpose, and had thus drawn Tissaphernes off to Caria, he himself invaded Lydia, where the capital the enemy's kingdom was situated, and having crushed those in command at that place, he obtained possession of the king's treasure.99

IX. On Quelling a Mutiny of Soldiers

1 When the consul, Aulus Manlius, had learned that the soldiers had formed a plot in their winter-quarters in Campania to murder their hosts and seize their property, he disseminated the report that they would winter next season in the same place. Having thus postponed the plans of the conspirators, he rescued Campania from peril, and, so soon as occasion offered, inflicted punishment on the guilty.100

2 When on one occasion legions of Roman soldiers had broken out in a dangerous mutiny, Lucius Sulla shrewdly restored sanity to the frenzied troops; for he ordered a sudden announcement to be made that the enemy were at hand, bidding a shout to be raised by those summoning the men to arms, and the trumpets to be sounded. Thus the mutiny was broken up by the union of all forces against the foe.

3 When the senate of Milan had been massacred by Pompey's troops, Pompey, fearing that he might cause a mutiny if he should call out the guilty alone, ordered certain ones who were innocent to come interspersed among the others. In this way the guilty came with less fear, because they had not been singled out, and so did not seem to be sent for in consequence of any wrong-doing; while those whose conscience was clear kept watch on the guilty, lest by the escape of these the innocent should be disgraced.

4 When certain legions of Gaius Caesar mutinied, and in such a way as to seem to threaten even the life of their commander, he concealed his fear, and, advancing straight to the soldiers, with grim visage, readily granted discharge to those asking it. But these men were no sooner discharged than penitence forced them to apologize to their commander and to pledge themselves to greater loyalty in future enterprises.101

X. How to Check an Unseasonable Demand for Battle

1 After Quintus Sertorius had learned by experience that he was by no means a match for the whole Roman army, in order to prove this to the barbarians also, who were rashly demanding

battle, he brought into their presence two horses, one very strong, the other very feeble. Then he brought up two youths of corresponding physique, one robust, the other slight. The stronger youth was commanded to pull out the entire tail of the feeble horse, while the slight youth was commanded to pull out the hairs of the strong horse one by one. Then, when the slight youth had succeeded in his task, while the strong one was still vainly struggling with the tail of the weak horse, Sertorius observed: "By this illustration I have exhibited to you, my men, the nature of the Roman cohorts. They are invincible to him who attacks them in a body; yet he who assails them by groups will tear and rend them."102

2 When the same Sertorius saw his men rashly demanding the signal for battle and thought them in danger of disobeying orders unless they should engage the enemy, he permitted a squadron of cavalry to advance to harass the foe. When these troops became involved in difficulties, he sent others to their relief, and thus rescued all, showing more safely, and without injury, what would have been the outcome of the battle they had demanded. After that he found his men most amenable.103

3 When Agesilaus, the Spartan, was fighting against the Thebans and had encamped on the bank of a stream, being aware that the forces of the enemy far outnumbered his own, and wishing therefore to keep his men from the desire of fighting, he announced that he had been bidden by a response of the gods to fight on high ground. Accordingly, posting a small guard on the bank, he withdrew to the hills. The Thebans, interpreting this as a mark of fear, crossed the stream, easily dislodged the defending troops, and, following the rest too eagerly, were defeated by a smaller force, owing to the difficulties of the terrain.104

4 Scorylo, a chieftain of the Dacians, though he knew that the Romans were torn with the dissensions of the civil wars, yet did not think he ought to venture on any enterprise against them, inasmuch as a foreign war might be the means of uniting the citizens in harmony. Accordingly he pitted two dogs in combat before the populace, and when they became engaged in a desperate encounter, exhibited a wolf to them. The dogs straightway abandoned their fury against each other and attacked the wolf. By this illustration, Scorylo kept the barbarians from a movement which could only have benefited the Romans.

XI. How to arouse an Army's Enthusiasm for battle

1 When the consuls Marcus Fabius and Gnaeus Manlius were warring against the Etruscans, and the soldiers mutinied against fighting, the consuls on their side feigned a policy of delay, until soldiers, wrought upon by the taunts of the enemy, demanded battle and swore to return from it victorious.105

2 Fulvius Nobilior, deeming it necessary to fight with a small force against a large army of the Samnites who were flushed with success, pretended that one legion of the enemy had been bribed by him to turn traitor; and to strengthen belief in this story, he commanded the tribunes, the "first rank,"106 and the centurions to contribute all the ready money they had, or any gold and silver, in order that the price might be paid the traitors at once. He promised that, when victory was achieved, he would give generous presents besides to those who contributed for this purpose. This assurance brought such ardour and confidence to the Romans that they straightway opened battle and won a glorious victory.

3 Gaius Caesar, when about to fight the Germans and their king, Ariovistus, at a time when his own men had been thrown into panic, called his soldiers together and declared to the assembly that on that day he proposed to employ the services of the tenth legion alone. In this way he caused the soldiers of this legion to be stirred by his tribute to their unique heroism, while the rest were overwhelmed with mortification to think that reputation for courage should rest with others.107

4 Quintus Fabius Maximus, since he knew full well that the Romans possessed a spirit of independence which was roused by insult, and since he expected nothing just or reasonable from the Carthaginians, sent envoys to Carthage to inquire about terms of peace. When the envoys brought back proposals full of injustice and arrogance, the army of the Romans was

stirred to combat.108

5 When Agesilaus, general of the Spartans, had his camp near the allied city of Orchomenos and learned that very many of his soldiers were depositing their valuables within the fortifications, he commanded the townspeople to receive nothing belonging to his troops, in order that his soldiers might fight with more spirit, when they realised that they must fight for all their possessions.109

6 Epaminondas, general of the Thebans, on one occasion, when about to engage in battle with the Spartans, acted as follows. In order that his soldiers might not only exercise their strength, but also be stirred by their feelings, he announced in an assembly of his men that the Spartans had resolved, in case of victory, to massacre all males, to lead the wives and children of those executed into bondage, and to raze Thebes to the ground. By this announcement the Thebans were so roused that they overwhelmed the Spartans at the first onset.110

7 When Leotychides, the Spartan admiral, was on the point of fighting a naval battle on the very day when the allies had been victorious, although he was ignorant of the fact, he nevertheless announced that he had received news of the victory of their side, in order that in this way he might find his men more resolute for the encounter.111

8 When two youths, mounted on horseback, appeared in the battle which Aulus Postumius fought with the Latins, Postumius roused the drooping spirits of his men by declaring that the strangers were Castor and Pollux. In this way he inspired them to fresh combat.112

9 Archidamus, the Spartan, when waging war against the Arcadians, set up weapons in camp, and ordered horses to be led around them secretly at night. In the morning, pointing to their tracks and claiming that Castor and Pollux had ridden through the camp, he convinced his men that the same gods would also lend them aid in the battle itself.113

10 On one occasion when Pericles, general of the Athenians, was about to engage in battle, noticing a grove from which both armies were visible, very dense and dark, but unoccupied and consecrated to Father Pluto, he took a man of enormous stature, made imposing by high buskins, purple robes, and flowing hair, and placed him in the grove, mounted high on a chariot drawn by gleaming white horses. This man was instructed to drive forth, when the signal for battle should be given, to call Pericles by name, and to encourage him by declaring that the gods were lending their aid to the Athenians. As a result, the enemy turned and fled almost before a dart was hurled.

11 Lucius Sulla, in order to make his soldiers readier for combat, pretended that the future was foretold him by the gods. His last act, before engaging in battle, was to pray, in the sight of his army, to a small image which he had taken from Delphi, entreating it to speed the promised victory.114

12 Gaius Marius had a certain wisewoman from Syria, from whom he pretended to learn in advance the outcome of battles.115

12 Quintus Sertorius, employing barbarian troops who were not amenable to reason, used to take with him through Lusitania a beautiful white deer, and claimed that from it he knew in advance what ought to be done, and what avoided. In this way he aimed to induce the barbarians to obey all his commands as though divinely inspired.116

[This sort of stratagem is to be used not merely in cases when we deem those to whom we apply it simple-minded, but much more when the ruse invented is such as might be thought to have been suggested by the gods.]

14 Alexander of Macedon on one occasion, when about to make sacrifice, used a preparation to inscribe certain letters on the hand which the priest was about to place beneath the vitals. These letters indicated that victory was vouchsafed to Alexander. When the steaming liver had received the impress of these characters and had been displayed by the king to the soldiers, the circumstances raised their spirits, since they thought that the god gave them assurance of victory.117

15 The soothsayer Sudines did the same thing when Eumenes was about to engage in battle with the Gauls.118

16 Epaminondas, the Theban in his contest against the Spartans, thinking that the confidence of his troops needed strengthening by an appeal to religious sentiment, removed by night the weapons which were attached to the decorations of the temples, and convinced his soldiers that the gods were attending his march, in order to lend their aid in the battle itself.119

17 Agesilaus, the Spartan, on one occasion captured certain Persians. The appearance of these people, when dressed in uniform, inspired great terror. But Agesilaus stripped his prisoners and exhibited them to his soldiers, in order that their delicate white bodies might excite contempt.120

18 Gelo, tyrant of Syracuse, having undertaken war against the Carthaginians, after taking many prisoners, stripped all the feeblest, especially from among the auxiliaries, who were very swarthy, and exhibited them nude before the eyes of his troops, in order to convince his men that their foes were contemptible.121

19 Cyrus, king of the Persians, wishing to rouse the ambition of his men, employed them an entire day in the fatiguing labour of cutting down a certain forest. Then on the following day he gave them a most generous feast, and asked them which they liked better. When they had expressed their preference for the feast, he said: "And yet it is only through the former that we can arrive at the latter; for unless you conquer the Medes, you cannot be free and happy." In this way he roused them to the desire for combat.122

20 Lucius Sulla, in the campaign against Archelaus, general of Mithridates, found his troops somewhat disinclined for battle at the Piraeus. But by imposing tiresome tasks upon his men he brought them to the point where they demanded the signal for battle of their own accord.123

21 Fabius Maximus, fearing that his troops would fight less resolutely in consequence of their reliance on their ships, to which it was possible to retreat, ordered the ships to be set on fire before the battle began.124

XII. On Dispelling the Fears Inspired in Soldiers by Adverse Omens

1 Scipio, having transported his army from Italy to Africa, stumbled as he was disembarking. When he saw the soldiers struck aghast at this, by his steadiness and loftiness of spirit he converted their cause of concern into one of encouragement, by saying: "Congratulate me, my men! I have hit Africa hard."125

2 Gaius Caesar, having slipped as he was about to embark on ship, exclaimed: "I hold thee fast, Mother Earth." By this interpretation of the incident he made it seem that he was destined to come back to the lands from which he was setting out.126

3 When the consul Tiberius Sempronius Gracchus was engaged in battle with the Picentines, a sudden earthquake threw both sides into panic. Thereupon Gracchus put new strength and courage into his men by urging them to attack the enemy while the latter were overwhelmed with superstitious awe. Thus he fell upon them and defeated them.127

4 Sertorius, when by a sudden prodigy the outsides of the shields of his cavalrymen and the breasts of their horses showed marks of blood, interpreted this as a mark of victory, since those were the parts which were wont to be spattered with the blood of the enemy.

5 Epaminondas, the Theban, when his soldiers were depressed because the decoration hanging from his spear like a fillet had been torn away by the wind and carried to the tomb of a certain Spartan, said: "Do not be concerned, comrades! Destruction is foretold for the Spartans. Tombs are not decorated except for funerals."128

5 The same Epaminondas, when a meteor fell from the sky by night and struck terror to the hearts of those who noticed it, exclaimed: "It is a light sent us from the powers above."

7 When the same Epaminondas was about to open battle against the Spartans, the chair on which he had sat down gave way beneath him, whereat all the soldiers, greatly troubled, interpreted this as an unlucky omen. But Epaminondas exclaimed: "Not at all; we are simply forbidden to sit."129

8 Gaius Sulpicius Gallus not only announced an approaching eclipse of the moon, in order to prevent the soldiers from taking it as a prodigy, but also gave the reasons and causes of the eclipse.130

9 When Agathocles, the Syracusan, was fighting against the Carthaginians, and his soldiers on the eve of battle were thrown into panic by a similar eclipse of the moon, which they interpreted as a prodigy, he explained the reason why this happened, and showed them that, whatever it was, it had to do with nature, and not with their own purposes.131

10 Pericles, when a thunderbolt struck his camp and terrified his soldiers, calling an assembly, struck fire by knocking two stones together in the sight of all his men. He thus allayed their panic by explaining that the thunderbolt was similarly produced by the contact of the clouds.

11 When Timotheus, the Athenian, was about to contend against the Corcyreans in a naval battle, his pilot, hearing one of the rowers sneeze, started to give the signal for retreat, just as the fleet was setting out; whereupon Timotheus exclaimed: "Do you think it strange if one out of so many thousands has had a chill?"132

12 As Chabrias, the Athenian, was about to fight a naval battle, a thunderbolt fell directly across the path of his ship. When the soldiers were filled with dismay at such a portent, he said: "Now is the very time to begin battle, when Jupiter, mightiest of the gods, reveals that his power is present with our fleet."133

The Editor's Notes:

1 Sextus Frontinus: The praenomen appears at the beginning of Book II in one MS., P.
2 I have undertaken to reduce to system the rules of military science: Frontinus alludes to his work on the Art of War. This is now lost.
3 Cato's memos: 195 B.C. Cf. Appian Hisp. 41.
4 Himilco's memos: 396 B.C. Cf. Polyaenus V.X.2.
5 Laelius' slave: 203 B.C. Cf. Liv. XXX.4.
6 Tarquin the Proud: The surname Superbus, here given to Tarquinius Priscus, the father, is usually applied only to his son, the last Roman king.
7 Tarquin's poppies: Cf. Liv. I.54; Val. Max. VII.IV.2. Herod. V.92 tells the same story of Periander and Thrasybulus.
8 the city: Alexandria.
9 Caesar's riotous living in Egypt: 48 B.C. Cf. Appian C. II.89.
10 Ventidius' tale of fears: Since Ventidius really wished the Parthians to take his longer route, that his reinforcement might have time to arrive, he led Pharnaeus to believe that he hoped they would cross by the shorter route. For he knew that Pharnaeus would counsel the Parthians to take the course of action not desired by himself.
11 bridge: The text is very uncertain at this point, though the general meaning is clear.
12 Ventidius and Pacorus: 38 B.C. Cf. Dio XLIX.19.
13 Mithridates' foraging and fires: 66 B.C. Cf. Appian Mithr. 98.
14 Domitian's census: 83 A.D.
15 Claudius Nero's phantom camp: 207 B.C. Cf. Val. Max. VII.IV.4; Livy XXVII.43 ff.
16 Themistocles plays sick: 478 B.C. Cf. Thuc. I.90 ff.
17 Metellus Pius' talking tunic: 79-72 B.C. Cf. Val. Max. VII.IV.5.
18 Crassus' deaf soldier: Plut. Demetr. 28 tells the same story of Antigonus and Demetrius.
19 After they had reported the results of their observations, the destruction of the camp by fire: i.e. the information furnished by the spies enabled Scipio to set fire to the camp of Syphax.
20 Scipio's loose horse: 203 B.C. Cf. Liv. XXX.4 ff.
21 Fabius Caeso spies on the Etruscans: 310 B.C. Cf. Liv. IX.36.
22 Hamilcar Rhodinus, fickle friend: 331 B.C. Cf. Justin. XXI.VI.1.
23 Cato tortures a soldier: 195 B.C. Plut. Cat. Maj. 13 attributes this stratagem to Cato at Thermopylae four years later.
24 the inner part: The letter was presumably in codex form, with the second and third leaves

fastened together by a special seal.
25 Marius' "don't read this": 104 B.C.
26 Aemilius Paulus at Vetulonia: Q. Aemilius Papus, consul in 282 and 278 B.C., waged war on the Etruscans. Pliny N. H. III.138 shows a like confusion of these names.

27 Tisamenus' birds: Cf. Polyaen. II.XXXVII.
28 Hasdrubal's thin horses: 207 B.C. Cf. I.I.9 and Livy XXVII.47.
29 Fabius Maximus' delaying: 217 B.C. Cf. Livy XXII.XII.6-12.
30 impatient Philip: 339 B.C. Cf. Justin IX.1.
31 Hasdrubal splits up his forces: 207 B.C. Cf. Livy XXVIII.2-3.
32 Themistocles' emergency preparations: 480 B.C. Cf. Herod. VIII.41.
33 Pericles' emergency preparations: 431 B.C. Cf. Thuc. I.143.
34 Scipio brings the war home to the Carthaginians: 204 B.C. Cf. Appian Hann. 55; Livy XXVIII.40 ff.
35 the Athenians bring the war home to the Spartans: 413 B.C. Cf. Thuc. VII.18.
36 Domitian extends the frontline: 83 A.D.
37 scorpion: A military engine for throwing darts, stones, and other missiles.
38 Aemilius Paulus' human shields: 282 B.C. Cf. Zonar. VIII.2. Since no Aemilius Paulus waged war with the Tarentines, this is probably the Papus referred to in the note to I.II.7.
39 Agesilaus' human shields: 396 B.C. Cf. Polyaen. II.I.30.
40 Agesilaus' feint towards Thebes: 394 or 377 B.C. Cf. Zen. Hell. V.IV.49 ff.; Polyaen. II.I.24.
41 Autophradates' false retreat: 359-330 B.C. Cf. Polyaen. VII.XXVII.1.
42 Philip's dilatory peace negotiations: 210 B.C.
43 Iphicrates' Seals: 389-388 B.C. Cf. Polyaen. III.IX.33.
44 Pompey's troops march around a lot: Cf. the Spartan trick at Aegospotami, Xen. Hell. II.I.21 ff.
45 Alexander crosses the Hydaspes: 326 B.C. Cf. Polyaen. IV.III.9; Plut. Alex. 60; Curt. VIII.13.5 ff.° Frontinus, misled by different names given to the river, probably took the same story from two different sources. Cf. Introd. p. xxv.°
46 Xenophon makes the Armenians run back and forth: 401 B.C. Cf. Xen. Anab. IV.III.20; Polyaen. I.XLIX.4.
47 Appius Claudius' constitutional war powers rumour: 264 B.C. Cf. Polyb. I.XI.9. Zonar. VIII.VIII.6 gives a somewhat different account of this crossing.
48 The Spartan navy disguises itself as Carthaginians: 397 B.C. Cf. Polyaen. II.XI.
49 the straits called Stena: i.e., the Hellespont.
50 Philip's disinformation: 340-339 B.C. Polyaen. IV.II.8 attributes this stratagem to Philip on the occasion of his march against Amphissa.
51 Philip's dilatory peace negotiations: 339 B.C.
52 Chabrias' lure: 388 B.C. Cf. Polyaen. III.XI.10, 12.
53 Quintus Sertorius' firewall: 80-72 B.C.
54 Pelopidas' firewall: 369-364 B.C. cf. Polyaen. II.IV.2.
55 Lutatius Catulus' phantom camp: 102 B.C.
56 Croesus diverts a river: 546 B.C. Cf. Herod. I.75.
57 Pompey fortifies Brundisium: 49 B.C. Cf. Caes. B.C. I.27-28.
58 Chained harbor no obstacle to Duilius: 260 B.C. Zonar. VIII.16 makes Hippo, rather than Syracuse, the scene of this stratagem.
59 harbour: Piraeus.
60 Lysander's ships on wheels: 404 B.C.
61 Hirtuleius' firewall: 79-75 B.C.
62 Caesar's stealthy retreat: 49 B.C. Cf. Caes. B.C. I.42.

63 Pericles' backdoor escape: 430 B.C. Cf. III.IX.9. Variations of the same story. Polyaen. V.X.3 attributes this stratagem to Himilco.
64 Lysimachus' troops dig trenches and fill them in: 323-281 B.C.
65 Publius Decius' diversion: 343 B.C. Cf. Liv. VII.34 ff.
66 Calpurnius Flamma's diversion: 258 B.C. Cf. Livy XXII.LX.11; Zonar. VIII.12. Gell. III.7 gives a different account of this incident.
67 Minucius' clumsy Numidians: 193 B.C. Cf. Livy XXXV.11.
68 Sulla's trumpeter: 90 B.C.
69 Sulla's truce: 92 B.C.
70 Hasdrubal's dilatory peace negotiations: 211 B.C. Cf. Livy XXVI.17; Zonar. IX.7.
71 Spartacus' bridge of corpses: 71 B.C.
72 Spartacus' wicker ropes: 73 B.C. Cf. Plut. Crassus 9; Flor. III.20.
73 Spartacus' corpses stand guard: 73 B.C.
74 Brasidas lets himself be surrounded: 424 or 422 B.C. Cf. Thuc. IV.102, 106 ff.; V.6-11.
75 Iphicrates' ambush: 389 B.C. This same story is told in II.XI.4. Cf. also Polyaen. III.IX.41, 46, 50.
76 Darius' dogs and donkeys: 513 B.C. Cf. Herod. IV.135; Polyaen. VII.XI.4.
77 Hannibal's flaming oxen: 217 B.C. Cf. Livy XXII.16-17; Appian Hann. 14-15.
78 large enough to cause delay: Thus giving him time to set this ambush.
79 quicken their pace and flee: i.e. to give the appearance of flight.
80 Iphicrates' rested troops: 389 B.C. Cf. Polyaen. III.IX.49, 54.
81 the Boii's falling timber: 216 B.C. Twenty-five thousand, according to Livy XXIII.24.
82 Metellus' elephant floaters: 250 B.C. Cf. Zonar. VIII.14.
83 Hannibal's recalcitrant elephants: 218 B.C. Cf. Livy XXI.XXVIII.5-12.
84 broom: The Spanish broom, used for making rope.
85 The Carthaginians make cordage: 146 B.C. Cf. Flor. II.XV.10.
86 Mark Anthony's bark shields: 43 B.C.
87 Spartacus' wicker shields: 73 B.C. Cf. Flor. III.XX.6.
88 Alexander leads his men: 332-331 B.C. Cf. Polyaen. IV.III.25. Curt. VII.V.9-12 and Plut Alex. 42 have a slightly different version.
89 Coriolanus' selective pillage: 489 B.C. Cf. Livy II.XXXIX.5-8; Plut. Coriol. 27.
90 Hannibal and Fabius' real estate: 217 B.C. Cf. Livy XXII.XXIII.1-8; Plut. Fab. 7. Polyaen. I.XXXVI.2 attributes a like act to Pericles.
91 Fabius Maximus divides the enemy: 295 B.C. Cf. Livy X.27.
92 Manius Curius' diversionary attacks: 290 B.C.
93 Titus Didius calls for battle: 98-93 B.C. In Spain.
94 The Romans undermine Hannibal's influence: 192 B.C. Cf. Livy XXXV.14; Nep. Hann. 2.
95 Metellus' letters to Jugurtha's advisers: 108 B.C. Cf. Sall. Jug. 61, 62, 70, 72.
96 Caesar breaks camp: 49 B.C. Cf. Caes. B.C. I.66.
97 Scipio intercepts Hannibal's reinforcements: 202 B.C. Cf. Appian Pun. 36.
98 Dionysius ties his enemies down: 396 B.C. Cf. Polyaen. V.II.9.
99 Agesilaus' disinformation: 395 B.C. Cf. Xen. Hell. III.IV.20; Plut. Ages. 9-10; Nep. Ages. 3.
100 Manlius foils a mutiny: Livy VII.38-39 attributes this stratagem to C. Marcius Rutilius, consul in 342 B.C.
101 Caesar forestalls a mutiny: 47 B.C. Cf. Suet. Caes. 70; Appian B. C. II.92.
102 Sertorius' horsetails: 80-72 B.C. Cf. Val. Max. VII.III.6; Plut. Sert. 16; Hor. Epist. II.I.45 ff.; Plin. Epist. III.IX.11.
103 Sertorius gives his men a taste of the battle they want: 80-72 B.C. Cf. Plut. Sert. 16.
104 Agesilaus listens to the gods: 369 B.C. Cf. Polyaen. II.1.27.

105 Fabius and Manlius let their troops sit on the sidelines: 480 B.C. Cf. Livy II.XLIII.11-xlv; Dionys. IX.7-10.
106 first rank: These were a special class of centurions.
107 Caesar chooses the tenth legion: 58 B.C. Cf. Caes. B.C. I.XXXIX.7, XL.1, 14 ff.
108 Fabius Maximus goes out and gets a bad treaty offer: 217-203 B.C.
109 Agesilaus prohibits safe deposits: Cf. Polyaen. II.I.18.
110 Epaminondas terrifies his own people: 371 B.C.

111 Leotychides' victory announcement: 479 B.C. Cf. Diodor. XI.34-35; Polyaen. I.33. Herod. IX.100-101 has a different version.
112 Aulus Postumius recognizes the Dioscuri: 496 B.C. Cf. Val. Max. I.VIII.1; Cic. De Nat. Deor. II.II.6; Dionys. VI.13.
113 Archidamus and the horses of the Dioscuri: 467 B.C. Cf. Polyaen. I.XLI.1.
114 Sulla's prayers: Cf. Val. Max. I.II.3; Plut. Sulla 29.
115 Marius' Syrian wisewoman: Cf. Val. Max. I.II.3a; Plut. Mar. 17; Gell. XV.22.
116 Sertorius' beautiful white deer: Cf. Val. Max. I.II.4; Plut. Sertor. 11; Gell. XV.22.
117 Alexander's favorable entrails: Cf. Polyaen. IV.III.14 and IV.XX. Plut. Apophth. Lacon. Ages. Magni 77 attributes this stratagem to Agesilaus.

118 Sudines' favorable entrails: Cf. Polyaen. IV.XX.
119 Epaminondas' statues prepare for battle: 371 B.C. Cf. Polyaen. II.III.8 and 12.
120 Agesilaus' naked prisoners: 395 B.C. Cf. Polyaen. II.I.16; Xen. Hell. III.IV.19; Plut. Ages. 9.
121 Gelo's naked prisoners, with a racial twist: 480 B.C.
Thayer's Note: This is one of the admittedly rare places in ancient sources that suggest that the Greeks and Romans were not so free of racial prejudices as current revisionism makes them out to be.
122 Cyrus' object lesson: 558 B.C. Cf. Herod. I.126; Polyaen. VII.VI.7; Justin. I.VI.4-6.
123 Sulla's work details: 86 B.C.
124 Fabius Maximus sets his own ships on fire: 315 B.C. Cf. Livy IX.23.
125 Scipio hits Africa hard: 204 B.C.

126 Caesar holds Earth: Cf. Suet. Caes. 59.
127 Tiberius Gracchus makes good use of an earthquake: P. Sempronius Sophus, consul, defeated the Picentines in 268 B.C. Cf. Flor. I.19.
128 Epaminondas on decorating tombs: 371 B.C. Cf. Diodor. XV.LII.5 ff.
129 we are forbidden to sit: i.e., "we must be up and doing."
130 Sulpicius Gallus explains an eclipse: 168 B.C. Cf. Livy XLIV.37; Cic. De Senect. xiv.49; Val. Max. VIII.XI.1.
131 Agathocles explains an eclipse: 310 B.C. Cf. Justin. XXII.VI.1-5; Diodor. XX.V.5.
132 Timotheus' sneezing rower: 375 B.C. Cf. Polyaen. III.X.2.
133 Chabrias' thunderbolt: 391-357 B.C.

Book II

Having in Book I given classes of examples which, as I believe, will suffice to instruct a general in those matters which are to be attended to before beginning battle, I will next in order present examples which bear on those things that are usually done in the battle itself, and then those that come subsequent to the engagement.

Of those which concern the battle itself, there are the following classes:

I. On choosing the time for battle.
II. On choosing the place for battle.
III. On the disposition of troops for battle.
IV. On creating panic in the enemy's ranks.
V. On ambushes.
VI. On letting the enemy escape, lest, brought to bay, he renew the battle in desperation.
VII. On concealing reverses.
VIII. On restoring morale by firmness.

Of the matters which deserve attention after battle, I consider that there are the following classes:

IX. On bringing the war to a close after a successful engagement.
X. On repairing one's losses after a reverse.
XI. On ensuring the loyalty of those whom one mistrusts.
XII. What to do for the defence of the camp, in case a commander lacks confidence in his present forces.
XIII. On retreating.

I. On choosing the time for battle

1 When Publius Scipio was in Spain and had learned that Hasdrubal, leader of the Carthaginians, had marched out and drawn up his troops in battle array early in the morning before they had had breakfast, he kept back his own men till one o'clock, having ordered them to rest and eat. When the enemy, exhausted with hunger, thirst, and waiting under arms, had begun to return to camp, Scipio suddenly led forth his troops, opened battle, and won the day.1

2 When Metellus Pius was waging war against Hirtuleius in Spain, and the latter had drawn up his troops immediately after daybreak and marched them against Metellus' entrenchments, Metellus held his own forces in camp till noon, as the weather at that time of year was extremely hot. Then, when the enemy were overcome by the heat, he easily defeated them, since his own men were fresh and their strength unimpaired.2

3 When the same Metellus had joined forces with Pompey against Sertorius in Spain, and had repeatedly offered battle, the enemy declined combat, deeming himself unequal to two. Later on, however, Metellus, noticing that the soldiers of the enemy, fired with great enthusiasm, were calling for battle, baring their arms, and brandishing their spears, thought it best to retreat betimes before their ardour. Accordingly he withdrew and caused Pompey to do the same.

4 When Postumius was in Sicily in his consulate, his camp was •three miles distant from the Carthaginians. Every day the Punic chieftains drew up their line of battle directly in front of the fortifications of the Romans, while Postumius offered resistance by way of constant

skirmishes, conducted by a small band before his entrenchments. As soon as the Carthaginian commander came to regard this as a matter of course, Postumius quietly made ready all the rest of his troops within the ramparts, meeting the assault of the force with a few, according to his former practice, but keeping them engaged longer than usual. When, after noon was past, they were retreating, weary and suffering from hunger, Postumius, with fresh troops, put them to rout, exhausted as they were by the aforementioned embarrassments.3

5 Iphicrates, the Athenian, having discovered that the enemy regularly ate at the same hour, commanded his own troops to eat at an earlier hour, and then led them out to battle. When the enemy came forth, he so detained them as to afford them no opportunity either of fighting or of withdrawing. Then, as the day drew to a close, he led his troops back, but nevertheless held them under arms. The enemy, exhausted both by standing in the line and by hunger, straightway hurried off to rest and eat, whereupon Iphicrates again led forth his troops, and finding the enemy disorganized, attacked their camp.4

6 When the same Iphicrates had his camp for several days near the Lacedaemonians, and each side was in the habit of going forth at a regular hour for forage and wood, he one day sent out slaves and camp-followers in the dress of soldiers for this service, holding back his fighting men; and as soon as the enemy had dispersed on similar errands, he captured their camp. Then as they came running back from all quarters to the mêlée, unarmed and carrying their bundles, he easily slew or captured them.5

7 When the consul Verginius, in the war with the Volscians, saw the enemy run forward at full stretch from a distance, he commanded his own men to keep steady and hold their javelins at rest. Then, when the enemy were out of breath, while his own army was still strong and fresh, he attacked and routed them.6

8 Since Fabius Maximus was well aware that the Gauls and Samnites were strong in the initial attack, while the tireless spirits of his own men actually waxed hotter as the struggle continued, he commanded his soldiers to rest content with holding the foe at the first encounter and to wear them out by delay. When this succeeded, bringing up reinforcements to his men in the van, and attacking with his full strength, he crushed and routed the enemy.7

9 At Chaeronea, Philip purposely prolonged the engagement, mindful that his own soldiers were seasoned by long experience, while the Athenians were ardent but untrained, and impetuous only in the charge. Then, as the Athenians began to grow weary, Philip attacked more furiously and cut them down.8

10 When the Spartans learned from scouts that the Messenians had broken out into such fury that they had come down to battle attended by their wives and children, they postponed the engagement.

11 In the Civil War, when Gaius Caesar held the army of Afranius and Petreius besieged and suffering from thirst, and when their troops, infuriated because of this, had slain all their beasts of burden9 and come out for battle, Caesar held back his own soldiers, deeming the occasion ill-suited for an engagement, since his opponents were so inflamed with wrath and desperation.10

12 Gnaeus Pompey, desiring to check the flight of Mithridates and force him to battle, chose night as the time for the encounter, arranging to block his march as he withdrew. Having made his preparations accordingly, he suddenly forced his enemy to fight. In addition to this, he so

drew up his force that the moonlight falling in the faces of the Pontic soldiers blinded their eyes, while it gave his own troops a distinct and clear view of the enemy.11

13 It is well known that Jugurtha, aware of the courage of the Romans, was always wont to engage in battle as the day was drawing to a close, so that, in case his men were routed, they might have the advantage of night for getting away.12

14 At Tigranocerta in Greater Armenia, Lucullus, in the campaign against Mithridates and Tigranes, did not have above 15,000 armed men, while the enemy had an innumerable host, which for this very reason was unwieldy. Taking advantage, accordingly, of this handicap of the foe, Lucullus attacked their line before it was in order, and straightway routed it so completely that even the kings themselves discarded their trappings and fled.13

15 In the campaign against the Pannonians, when the barbarians in warlike mood had formed for battle at the very break of day, Tiberius Nero held back hand his own troops, and allowed the enemy to be hampered by the fog and be drenched with the showers, which happened to be frequent that day. Then, when he noticed that they were weary with standing, and faint not only from exposure but also from exhaustion, he gave the signal, attacked and defeated them.14

16 Gaius Caesar, when in Gaul, learned that it was a principle and almost a law with Ariovistus, king of the Germans, not to fight when the moon was waning. Caesar therefore chose that time above all others for engaging in battle, when the enemy were embarrassed by their superstition, and so conquered them.15

17 The deified Vespasian Augustus attacked Jews on their sabbath, a day on which it is sinful for them to do any business, and so defeated them.16

18 When Lysander, the Spartan, was fighting against the Athenians at Aegospotami, he began by attacking the vessels of the Athenians at a regular hour and then calling off his fleet. After this had become an established procedure, as the Athenians on one occasion, after his withdrawal, were dispersing to collect their troops, he deployed his fleet as usual and withdrew it. Then, when most of the enemy had scattered according to their wont, he attacked and slew the rest, and captured all their vessels.17

II. On Choosing the Place for Battle

1 Manius Curius, observing that the phalanx of King Pyrrhus could not be resisted when in extended order, took pains to fight in confined quarters, where the phalanx, being massed together, would embarrass itself.18

2 In Cappadocia Gnaeus Pompey chose a lofty site for his camp. As a result the elevation so assisted the onset of his troops that he easily overcame Mithridates by the sheer weight of his assault.19

3 When Gaius Caesar was about to contend with Pharnaces, son of Mithridates, he drew up his line of battle on a hill. This move made victory easy for him, since the darts, hurled from higher ground against the barbarians charging from below, straightway put them to flight.20

4 When Lucullus was planning to fight Mithridates and Tigranes at Tigranocerta in Greater Armenia, he himself swiftly gained the level top of the nearest hill with a part of his troops, and then rushed down upon the enemy posted below, at the same time attacking their cavalry

on the flank. When the cavalry broke and straightway threw the infantry into confusion, Lucullus followed after them and gained a most notable victory.21

5 Ventidius, when fighting against the Parthians, would not lead out his soldiers until the Parthians were within five hundred paces. Thus by a rapid advance he came so near them that, meeting them at close quarters, he escaped their arrows, which they shoot from a distance. By this scheme, since he exhibited a certain show of confidence, he quickly subdued the barbarians.22

6 At Numistro, when Hannibal was expecting a battle with Marcellus, he secured a position where his flank was protected by hollows and precipitous roads. By thus making the ground serve as a defence, he won a victory over a most renowned commander.23

7 Again at Cannae, when Hannibal learned that the Volturnus River, at variance with the nature of other streams, sent out high winds in the morning, which carried swirling sand and dust, he so marshalled his line of battle that the entire fury of the elements fell on the rear of his own troops, but struck the Romans in the face and eyes. Since this difficulty was a serious obstacle to the enemy, he won that memorable victory.24

8 After Marius had settled on a day for fighting the Cimbrians and Teutons, he fortified his soldiers with food and stationed them in front of his camp, in order that the army of the enemy might be exhausted by marching over the interval between the opposing armies. Then, when the enemy were thus used up, he confronted them with another embarrassment by so arranging his own line of battle that the barbarians were caught with the sun and wind and dust in their faces.25

9 When Cleomenes, the Spartan, in his battle against Hippias, the Athenian, found that the latter's main strength lay in his cavalry, he thereupon felled trees and cluttered the battlefield with them, thus making it impassable for cavalry.26

10 The Iberians in Africa, upon encountering a great multitude of foes and fearing that they would be surrounded, drew near a river which at that point flowed along between deep banks. Thus, defended by the river in the rear and enabled by their superior prowess to make frequent onsets upon those nearest them, they routed the entire host of their adversaries.

11 Xanthippus, the Spartan, by merely changing the locality of operations, completely altered the fortunes of the Punic War; for when, summoned as a mercenary by the despairing Carthaginians, he had noticed that the Africans, who were superior in cavalry and elephants, kept to the hills, while the Romans, whose strength was in their infantry, held to the plains, he brought the Carthaginians down to level ground, where he broke the ranks of the Romans with the elephants. Then pursuing their scattered troops with Numidians, he routed their army, which till that day had been victorious on land and sea.27

12 Epaminondas, leader of the Thebans, when about to marshal his troops in battle array against the Spartans, ordered his cavalry to engage in manoeuvres along the front. Then, when he had filled the eyes of the enemy with clouds of dust and had caused them to expect an encounter with cavalry, he led his infantry around to one side, where it was possible to attack the enemy's rear from higher ground, and thus, by a surprise attack, cut them to pieces.28

13 Against a countless horde of Persians, three hundred Spartans seized and held the pass of Thermopylae which was capable of admitting only a like number of hand-to-hand opponents. In consequence, the Spartans became numerically equal to the barbarians, so far as opportunity

for fighting was concerned, and being superior to them in valour, slew large numbers of them. Nor would they have been overcome, had not the enemy been led around to the rear by the traitor Ephialtes, the Trachinian, and thus been enabled to overwhelm them.29

14 Themistocles, leader of the Athenians, saw that it was most advantageous for Greece to fight in the Straits of Salamis against the vast numbers of Xerxes's vessels, but he was unable to persuade his fellow Athenians of this. He therefore employed a stratagem to make the barbarians force the Greeks to do what was advantageous for the latter; for under pretence of turning traitor, he sent a messenger to Xerxes to inform him that the Greeks were planning flight, and that the situation would be more difficult for the King if he should besiege each city separately. By this policy, in the first place he caused the host of the barbarians to be kept on the alert doing guard-duty all night; in the second place, he made it possible for his own followers, the next morning, with strength unimpaired, to encounter the barbarians all exhausted with watching, and (precisely as he had wished) in a confined place, where Xerxes could not utilise his superiority in numbers.30

III. On the Disposition of Troops for Battle

1 Gnaeus Scipio, when campaigning in Spain against Hanno, near the town of Indibile, noted that the Carthaginian line of battle was drawn up with the Spaniards posted on the right wing — sturdy soldiers, to be sure, but fighting for others — while on the left were the less powerful, but more resolute, Africans. He accordingly drew back his own left wing, and keeping his battle-line at an angle with the enemy, engaged the enemy with his right wing, which he had formed of his sturdiest soldiers. Then routing the Africans and putting them to flight, he easily forced the surrender of the Spaniards, who had stood apart after the manner of spectators.31

2 When Philip, king of the Macedonians, was waging war against the Hyllians,32 he noticed that the front of the enemy consisted entirely of men picked from the whole army, while their flanks were weaker. Accordingly he placed the stoutest of his own men on the right wing, attacked the enemy's left, and by throwing their whole line into confusion won a complete victory.33

3 Pammenes, the Theban, having observed the battle-line of the Persians, where the most powerful troops were posted on the right wing, drew up his own men also on the same plan, putting all his cavalry and the bravest of his infantry on the right wing, but stationing opposite the bravest of the enemy his own weakest troops, whom he directed to flee at the first onset of the foe and to retreat to rough, wooded places. When in this way he had made the enemy's strength of no effect, he himself with the best part of his own forces enveloped the whole array of the enemy with his right wing and put them to rout.34

4 Publius Cornelius Scipio, who subsequently received the name Africanus, on one occasion, when waging war in Spain against Hasdrubal, leader of the Carthaginians, led out his troops day after day in such formation that the centre of his battle-line was composed of his best fighting men. But when the enemy also regularly came out marshalled on the same plan, Scipio, on the day when he had determined to fight, altered the scheme of his arrangement and stationed his strongest troops on the wings, having his light-armed troops in the centre, but slightly behind the line. Thus, by attacking the enemy's weakest point in crescent formation from the flank, where he himself was strongest, he easily routed them.35

5 Metellus, in the battle in which he vanquished Hirtuleius in Spain, had discovered that the battalions of Hirtuleius which were deemed strongest were posted in the centre. Accordingly

he drew back the centre of his own troops, to avoid encountering the enemy at that part of the line, until by an enveloping movement of his wings he could surround their centre from all sides.36

6 Artaxerxes, having superior numbers in his campaign against the Greeks, who had invaded Persia, drew up his line of battle with a wider front than the enemy, placing infantry, cavalry, and light-armed troops on the wings. Then by purposely causing the centre to advance more slowly he enveloped the enemy troops and cut them to pieces.37

7 On the other hand, at Cannae Hannibal, having drawn back his flanks and advanced his centre, drove back our troops at the first assault. Then, when the fighting began, and the flanks gradually worked towards each other moving forward according to instructions, Hannibal enveloped within his own lines the impetuously attacking enemy, forced them towards the centre from both sides, and cut them to pieces, using veteran troops of long training; for hardly anything but a trained army, responsive to every direction, can carry out this sort of tactics.38

8 In the Second Punic War, when Hasdrubal was seeking to avoid the necessity of an engagement, and had drawn up his line on a rough hillside behind protective works, Livius Salinator and Claudius Nero diverted their own forces to the flanks, leaving their centre vacant. Having in this way enveloped Hasdrubal, they attacked and defeated him.39

9 After Hannibal had been defeated in frequent battles by Claudius Marcellus, he finally laid out his camp on this plan: Protected by mountains, marshes, or similar advantages of terrain, he so posted his troops as to be able to withdraw his army, practically without loss, within his fortifications, in case the Romans won, but so as to have free option of pursuit, in case they gave way.

10 Xanthippus, the Spartan, in the campaign conducted p113in Africa against Marcus Atilius Regulus, placed his light-armed troops in the front line, holding the flower of his army in reserve. Then he directed the auxiliary troops,40 after hurling their javelins, to give way before the enemy, withdraw within the ranks of their fellow-soldiers, hurry to the flanks, and from there again rush forward to attack. Thus when the enemy had been met by the stronger troops, they were enveloped also by these light-armed forces.41

11 Sertorius employed the same tactics in Spain in the campaign against Pompey.42

12 Cleandridas, the Spartan, when fighting against the Lucanians, drew up his troops in close array, so as to present the appearance of a much smaller army. Then, when the enemy had thus been put off their guard, at the moment the engagement began he opened up his ranks, enveloped the enemy on the flank, and put them to rout.43

13 Gastron, the Spartan, having come to assist the Egyptians against the Persians, and realizing that the Greek soldiers were more powerful and more dreaded by the Persians, interchanged the arms of the two contingents, placing the Greeks in the front line. When these merely held their own in the encounter, he sent in the Egyptians as reinforcements. Although the Persians had proved equal to the Greeks (deeming them Egyptians), they gave way, so soon as they were set upon by a multitude, of whom (as supposedly consisting of Greeks) they had stood in terror.44

14 When Gnaeus Pompey was fighting in Albania, and the enemy were superior in numbers and in cavalry, he directed his infantry to cover their helmets, in order to avoid being visible in consequence of the reflection, and to take their place in a defile by a hill. Then he commanded

his cavalry to advance on the plain and to act as a screen to the infantry, but to withdraw at the first onset of the enemy, and, as soon as they had reached the infantry, to disperse to the flanks. When this manoeuvre had been executed, suddenly the force of infantry rose up, revealing its position, and pouring with unexpected attack upon the enemy who were heedlessly bent on pursuit, thus cut them to pieces.45

15 When Mark Antony was engaged in battle with the Parthians and these were showering his army with innumerable arrows, he ordered his men to stop and form a testudo.46 The arrows passed over this without harm to the soldiers, and the enemy's supply was soon exhausted.47

16 When Hannibal was contending against Scipio in Africa, having an army of Carthaginians and auxiliaries, part of whom were not only of different nationalities, but actually consisted of Italians, he placed eighty elephants in the forefront, to throw the enemy into confusion. Behind these he stationed auxiliary Gauls, Ligurians, Balearians, and Moors, that these might be unable to run away, since the Carthaginians were standing behind them, and in order that, being placed in front, they might at least harass the enemy, if not do him damage. In the second line he placed his own countrymen and the Macedonians, to be fresh to meet the exhausted Romans; and in the rear the Italians, whose loyalty he distrusted and whose indifference he feared, inasmuch as he had dragged most of them from Italy against their will.

Against this formation Scipio drew up the flower of his legions in three successive front lines, arranged according to hastati, principes, and triarii,48 not making the cohorts touch, but leaving a space between the detached companies through which the elephants driven by the enemy might easily be allowed to pass without throwing the ranks into confusion. These intervals he filled with light-armed skirmishers, that the line might show no gaps, giving them instructions to withdraw to the rear or the flanks at the first onset of the elephants. The cavalry he distributed on the flanks, placing Laelius in charge of the Roman horsemen on the right, and Masinissa in charge of the Numidians on the left. This shrewd scheme of arrangement was undoubtedly the cause of his victory.49

17 In the battle against Lucius Sulla, Archelaus placed his scythe-bearing chariots in front, for the purpose of throwing the enemy into confusion; in the second line he posted the Macedonian phalanx, and in the third line auxiliaries armed after the Roman way, with a sprinkling of Italian runaway slaves, in whose doggedness he had the greatest confidence. In the last line he stationed the light-armed troops, while on the two flanks, for the purpose of enveloping the enemy, he placed the cavalry, of whom he had a great number.

To meet these dispositions, Sulla constructed trenches of great breadth on each flank, and at their ends built strong redoubts. By this device he avoided the danger of being enveloped by the enemy, who outnumbered him in infantry and especially in cavalry. Next he arranged a triple line of infantry, leaving intervals through which to send, according to need, the light-armed troops and the cavalry, which he placed in the rear. He then commanded the postsignani,50 who were in the second line, to drive firmly into the ground large numbers stakes set close together, and as the chariots drew near, he withdrew the line of antesignani51 within these stakes. Then at length he ordered the skirmishers and light-armed troops to raise a general battle-cry and discharge their spears. By these tactics either the chariots of the enemy were caught among the stakes, or their drivers became panic-stricken at the din and were driven by the javelins back upon their own men, throwing the formation of the Macedonians into confusion. As these gave way, Sulla pressed forward, and Archelaus met him with cavalry, whereupon the Roman horsemen suddenly darted forth, drove back the enemy, and achieved victory.52

18 In the same way Gaius Caesar met the scythe-bearing chariots of the Gauls with stakes driven in the ground, and kept them in check.

19 At Arbela, Alexander, fearing the numbers of the enemy, yet confident in the valour of his own troops, drew up a line of battle facing in all directions, in order that his men, if surrounded, might be able to fight from all sides.53

20 When Perseus, king of the Macedonians, had drawn up a double phalanx of his own troops and had placed them in the centre of his forces, with light-armed troops on each side and cavalry on both flanks, Paulus in the battle against him drew up a triple array in wedge formation, sending out skirmishers every now and then between the wedges. Seeing nothing accomplished by these tactics, he determined to retreat, in order by this feint to lure the enemy after him on to rough ground, which he had selected with this in view. When even then the enemy, suspecting his ruse in retiring, followed in good order, he commanded the cavalry on the left wing to ride at full speed past the front of the phalanx, covering themselves with their shields, in order that the points of the enemy's spears might be broken by the shock of their encounter with the shields. When the Macedonians were deprived of their spears, they broke and fled.54

21 Pyrrhus, when fighting in defence of the Tarentines near Asculum, following the Homeric verse,55 according to which the poorest troops are placed in the centre, stationed Samnites and Epirotes on the right flank, Bruttians, Lucanians, and Sallentines on the left, with the Tarentines in the centre, ordering the cavalry and elephants to be held as reserves.

The consuls, on the other hand, very judiciously distributed their cavalry on the wings, posting legionary soldiers in the first line and in reserve, with auxiliary troops scattered among them. We are informed that there were forty thousand men on each side. Half of Pyrrhus's army was lost; on the Roman side only five thousand.56

22 In the battle against Caesar at Old Pharsalus,57 Gnaeus Pompey drew up three lines of battle, each one ten men deep, stationing on the wings and in the centre the legions upon whose prowess he could most safely rely, and filling the spaces between these with raw recruits. On the right flank he placed six hundred horsemen, along the Enipeus River, which with its channel and deposits had made the locality impassable; the rest of the cavalry he stationed on the left, together with the auxiliary troops, that from this quarter he might envelop the troops of Caesar.

Against these dispositions, Gaius Caesar also drew up a triple line, placing his legions in front and resting his left flank on marshes in order to avoid envelopment. On the right he placed his cavalry, among whom he distributed the fleetest of his foot-soldiers, men trained in cavalry fighting.58 Then he held in reserve six cohorts for emergencies, placing them obliquely on the right, from which quarter he was expecting an attack of the enemy's cavalry. No circumstance contributed more than this to Caesar's victory on that day; for as soon as Pompey's cavalry poured forth, these cohorts routed it by an unexpected onset, and delivered it up to the rest of the troops for slaughter.59

23 The Emperor Caesar Augustus Germanicus,60 when the Chatti, by fleeing into the forests, again and again interfered with the course of a cavalry engagement, commanded his men, as soon as they should reach the enemy's baggage-train, to dismount and fight on foot. By this means he made sure that his success should not be blocked by any difficulties of terrain.61

24 When Gaius Duellius saw that his own heavy ships were eluded by the mobile fleet of the Carthaginians and that the valour of his soldiers was thus brought to naught, he devised a kind of grappling-hook. When this caught hold of an enemy ship, the Romans, laying gangways over the bulwarks, went on board and slew the enemy in hand-to‑hand combat on their own vessels.62

IV. On creating panic in the enemy's ranks

1 When Papirius Cursor, the son,63 in his consulship failed to win any advantage in his battle against the stubbornly resisting Samnites, he gave no intimation on his purpose to his men, but commanded Spurius Nautius to arrange to have a few auxiliary horsemen and grooms, mounted on mules and trailing branches over the ground, race down in great commotion from a hill running at an angle with the field. As soon as these came in sight, he proclaimed that his colleague64 was at hand, crowned with victory, and urged his men to secure for themselves the glory of the present battle before he should arrive. At this the Romans rushed forward, kindling with confidence, while the enemy, disheartened at the sight of the dust, turned and fled.65

2 Fabius Rullus Maximus, when in Samnium in his fourth consulship, having vainly essayed in every way to break through the line of the enemy, finally withdrew the hastati66 from the ranks and sent them round with his lieutenant Scipio, under instructions to seize a hill from which they could rush down upon the rear of the enemy. When this had been done, the courage of the Romans rose, and the Samnites, fleeing in terror, were cut to pieces.67

3 The general Minucius Rufus, hard pressed by the Scordiscans and Dacians, for whom he was no match in numbers, sent his brother and a small squadron of cavalry on ahead, along with a detachment of trumpeters, directing him, as soon as he should see the battle begin, to show himself suddenly from the opposite quarter and to order the trumpeters to blow their horns. Then, when the hill-tops re-echoed with the sound, the impression of a huge multitude was borne in upon the enemy, who fled in terror.68

4 The consul Acilius Glabrio, when confronted by the army of King Antiochus, which the latter had drawn up in front of the Pass of Thermopylae in Greece, was not only hampered by the difficulties of terrain, but would have been repulsed with loss besides, had not Porcius Cato prevented this. Cato, although an ex-consul, was in the army as a tribune of the soldiers, elected to this office by the people. [Having been sent by Glabrio to make a détour], he dislodged the Aetolians, who were guarding the crest of Mt. Callidromus, and then suddenly appeared from the rear on the summit of a hill commanding the camp of the king. The forces of Antiochus were thus thrown into panic, whereupon the Romans attacked them from front and rear, repulsed and scattered the enemy, and captured their camp.69

5 The consul Gaius Sulpicius Peticus, when about to fight against the Gauls, ordered certain muleteers secretly to withdraw with their mules to the hills nearby, and then, after the engagement began, to exhibit themselves repeatedly to the combatants, as though mounted on horses. The Gauls, therefore, imagining that reinforcements were coming, fell back before the Romans, though already almost victorious.70

6 At Aquae Sextiae, Marius, purposing to fight a decisive battle with the Teutons on the morrow, sent Marcellus by night with a small detachment of horse and foot to the rear of the enemy, and, to complete the illusion of a large force, ordered armed grooms and camp-followers to go along with them, and also a large part of the pack-animals, wearing saddle-cloths, in order by this means to present the appearance of cavalry. He commanded these men

to fall upon the enemy from the rear, as soon as they should notice that the engagement had begun. This scheme struck such terror into the enemy that despite their great ferocity they turned and fled.71

7 Licinius Crassus in the Slave War, when about to lead forth his troops at Camalatrum against Castus and Cannicus, the leaders of the Gauls, sent twelve cohorts around behind the mountain with Gaius Pomptinius and Quintus Marcius Rufus, his lieutenants. When the engagement began, these troops, raising a shout, poured down the mountain in the rear, and so routed the enemy that they fled in all directions with no attempt at battle.72

8 Marcus Marcellus on one occasion, fearing that a feeble battle-cry would reveal the small number of his forces, commanded that sutlers, servants, and camp-followers of every sort should join in the cry. He thus threw the enemy into panic by giving the appearance of having a larger army.73

9 Valerius Laevinus, in the battle against Pyrrhus, killed a common soldier, and, holding up his dripping sword, made both armies believe that Pyrrhus had been slain. The enemy, therefore, panic-stricken at the falsehood, and thinking that they had been rendered helpless by the death of their commander, betook themselves in terror back to camp.74

10 In his struggle against Gaius Marius in Numidia, Jugurtha, having acquired facility in the use of the Latin language as a result of his early association with Roman camps, ran forward to the front line and shouted that he had slain Gaius Marius, thus causing many of our men to flee.75

11 Myronides, the Athenian, in an indecisive battle which he was waging against the Thebans, suddenly darted forward to the right flank of his own troops and shouted that he had already won victory on the left. Thus, by inspiring courage in his own men and fear in the enemy, he gained the day.76

12 Against overwhelming forces of the enemy's cavalry Croesus once opposed a troop of camels. At the strange appearance and smell of these beasts, the horses were thrown into panic, and not merely threw their riders, but also trampled the ranks of their own infantry under foot, thus delivering them into the hands of the enemy to defeat.77

13 Pyrrhus, king of the Epirotes, fighting on behalf of the Tarentines against the Romans, employed elephants in the same way, in order to throw the Roman army into confusion.78

14 The Carthaginians also often did the same thing in their battles against the Romans.79

15 The Volscians having on one occasion pitched their camp near some brush and woods, Camillus set fire to everything which would carry the conflagration up to their entrenchments, and thus deprived his adversaries of their camp.

16 In the same way, Publius Crassus in the Social War narrowly escaped being cut off with all his forces.

17 The Spaniards, when fighting against Hamilcar, hitched steers to carts and placed them in the front line. These carts they filled with pitch, tallow, and sulphur, and when the signal for battle was given, set them afire. Then, driving the steers against the enemy, they threw the line into panic and broke through.80

18 The Faliscans and Tarquinians disguised a number of men as priests, and had them hold torches and snakes in front of them, like Furies. Thus they threw the army of the Romans into panic.81

19 On one occasion the men of Veii and Fidenae snatched up torches and did the same thing.82

20 When Atheas, king of the Scythians, was contending against the more numerous tribe of the Triballi, he commanded that herds of asses and cattle should be brought up in the rear of the enemy's forces by women, children, and all the non-combatant population, and that spears, held aloft, should be carried in front of these. Then he spread abroad the rumour that reinforcements were coming to him from the more distant Scythian tribes. By this declaration he forced the enemy to withdraw.83

V. On Ambushes

1 Romulus, when he had drawn near to Fidenae, distributed a portion of his troops in ambush, and pretended to flee. When the enemy recklessly followed, he led them on to the point where he was holding his men in hiding, whereupon the latter, attacking from all sides, and taking the enemy off their guard, cut them to pieces in their onward rush.84

2 The consul Quintus Fabius Maximus, having been sent to aid the Sutrians against the Etruscans, caused the full brunt of the enemy's attack to fall upon himself. Then, feigning fear, he retired to higher ground, as though in retreat, and when the enemy rushed upon him pell-mell he attacked, and not merely defeated them in battle but captured their camp.85

3 Sempronius Gracchus, when waging war against the Celtiberians, feigned fear and kept his army in camp. Then, by sending out light-armed troops to harass the enemy and retreat forthwith, he caused the enemy to come out; whereupon he attacked them before they could form, and crushed them so completely that he also captured their camp.86

4 When the consul Lucius Metellus was waging war in Sicily against Hasdrubal — and with all the more alertness because of Hasdrubal's immense army and his one hundred and thirty elephants — he withdrew his troops, under pretence of fear, inside Panormus87 and constructed in front a trench of huge proportions. Then, observing Hasdrubal's army, with the elephants in the front rank, he ordered the hastati to hurl their javelins at the beasts and straightway to retire within their defences. The drivers of the elephants, enraged at such derisive treatment, drove the elephants straight towards the trench. As soon as the beasts were brought up to this, part were dispatched by a shower of darts, part were driven back to their own side, and threw the entire host into confusion. Then Metellus, who was biding his time, burst forth with his whole force, attacked the Carthaginians on the flank, and cut them to pieces. Besides this, he captured the elephants themselves.88

5 When Thamyris, queen of the Scythians, and Cyrus, king of the Persians, became engaged in an indecisive combat, the queen, feigning fear, lured Cyrus into a defile well-known to her own troops, and there, suddenly facing about, and aided by the nature of the locality, won a complete victory.89

6 The Egyptians, when about to engage in battle on a plain near a marsh, covered the marsh with seaweed, and then, when the battle began, feigning flight, drew the enemy into a trap; for the latter, while advancing too swiftly over the unfamiliar ground, were caught in the mire and surrounded.

7 Viriathus, who from being a bandit became leader of the Celtiberians, on one occasion, while pretending to give way before the Roman cavalry, led them on to a place full of deep holes. There, while he himself made his way out by familiar paths that afforded good footing, the Romans, ignorant of the locality, sank in the mire and were slain.90

8 Fulvius, commander in the Cimbrian war, having pitched his camp near the enemy, ordered his cavalry to approach the fortifications of the barbarians and to withdraw in pretended flight, after making an attack. When he had done this for several days, with the Cimbrians in hot pursuit, he noticed that their camp was regularly left exposed. Accordingly, maintaining his usual practice with part of his force, he himself, with light-armed troops, secretly took a position behind the camp of the enemy, and as they poured forth according to their custom, he suddenly attacked and demolished the unguarded rampart and captured their camp.91

9 Gnaeus Fulvius, when a force of Faliscans far superior to ours had encamped on our territory, had his soldiers set fire to certain buildings at a distance from the camp, in order that the Faliscans, thinking their own men had done this, might scatter in hope of plunder.

10 Alexander, the Epirote, when waging war against the Illyrians, first placed a force in ambush, and then dressed up some of his own men in Illyrian garb, ordering them to lay waste his own, that is to say, Epirote territory. When the Illyrians saw that this was being done, they themselves began to pillage right and left — the more confidently since they thought that those who led the way were scouts. But when they had been designedly brought by the latter into a disadvantageous position, they were routed and killed.

11 Leptines, the Syracusan, also, when waging war against the Carthaginians, ordered his own lands to be laid waste and certain farm-houses and forts to be set on fire. The Carthaginians, thinking this was done by their own men, went out themselves also to help; whereupon they were set upon by men lying in wait, and were put to rout.92

12 Maharbal,93 sent by the Carthaginians against rebellious Africans, knowing that the tribe was passionately fond of wine, mixed a large quantity of wine with mandragora, which in potency is something between a poison and a soporific. Then after an insignificant skirmish he deliberately withdrew. At dead of night, leaving in the camp some of his baggage and all the drugged wine, he feigned flight. When the barbarians captured the camp and in a frenzy of delight greedily drank the drugged wine, Maharbal returned, and either took them prisoners or slaughtered them while they lay stretched out as if dead.94

13 Hannibal, on one occasion, aware that both his own camp and that of the Romans were in places deficient in wood, deliberately abandoned the district, leaving many herds of cattle within his camp. The Romans, securing possession of these as booty, gorged themselves with flesh, which, owing to the scarcity of firewood, was raw and indigestible. Hannibal, returning by night with his army, finding them off their guard and gorged with raw meat, inflicted great loss upon them.

14 Tiberius Gracchus, when in Spain, upon learning that the enemy were suffering from lack of provisions, provided his camp with an elaborate supply of eatables of all kinds and then abandoned it. When the enemy had got possession of the camp and had gorged themselves to repletion with the food they found, Gracchus brought back his army and suddenly crushed them.95

15 The Chians, when waging war against the Erythreans, caught an Erythrean spy on a lofty eminence and put him to death. They then gave his clothes to one of their own soldiers, who, by giving a signal from the same eminence, lured the Erythreans into an ambush.

16 The Arabians, since their custom of giving notice of the arrival of the enemy by means of smoke by day, and by fire at night, was well known, issued orders on one occasion that these practices should continue without interruption until the enemy actually approached, when they should be discontinued. The enemy, imagining from the absence of the fires that their approach was unknown, advanced too eagerly and were overwhelmed.

17 Alexander of Macedon, when the enemy had fortified their camp on a lofty wooded eminence, withdrew a portion of his forces, and commanded those whom he left to kindle fires as usual, and thus to give the impression of the complete army. He himself, leading his forces around through untravelled regions, attacked the enemy and dislodged them from their commanding position.96

18 Memnon, the Rhodian, being superior in cavalry, and wishing to draw down to the plains an enemy who clung to the hills, sent certain of his soldiers under the guise of deserters to the camp of the enemy, to say that the army of Memnon was inspired with such a serious spirit of mutiny that some portion of it was constantly deserting. To lend credit to this assertion, Memnon ordered small redoubts to be fortified here and there in view of the enemy, as though the disaffected were about to retire to these. Inveigled by these representations, to who had been keeping themselves on the hills came down to level ground, and, as they attacked the redoubts, were surrounded by the cavalry.97

19 When Harrybas, king of the Molossians, was attacked in war by Bardylis, the Illyrian, who commanded a considerably larger army, he dispatched the non-combatant portion of his subjects to the neighbouring district of Aetolia, and spread the report that he was yielding up his towns and possessions to the Aetolians. He himself, with those who could bear arms, placed ambuscades here and there on the mountains and in other inaccessible places. The Illyrians, fearful lest the possessions of the Molossians should be seized by the Aetolians, began to race along in disorder, in their eagerness for plunder. As soon as they became scattered, Harrybas, emerging from his concealment and taking them unawares, routed them and put them to flight.

20 Titus Labienus, lieutenant of Gaius Caesar, eager to engage in battle with the Gauls before the arrival of the Germans, who, he knew, were coming to their aid, pretended discouragement, and, pitching his camp across the stream, announced his departure for the following day. The Gauls, imagining that he was in flight, began to cross the intervening river. Labienus, facing about with his troops, cut the Gauls to pieces in the very midst of their difficulties of crossing.98

21 Hannibal, on one occasion, learned that the camp of Fulvius, the Roman commander, was carelessly fortified and that Fulvius himself was taking many rash chances besides. Accordingly, at daybreak, when dense mists afforded cover, he permitted a few of his horsemen to show themselves to the sentries of our fortifications; whereupon Fulvius suddenly advanced. Meanwhile, Hannibal, at a different point, entered Fulvius's camp, and overwhelming the Roman rear, slew eight thousand of the bravest soldiers along with their commander himself.99

22 Once, when the Roman army had been divided between the dictator Fabius and Minucius, master of the horse, and Fabius was watching for a favourable opportunity, while Minucius

was burning with eagerness for battle, the same Hannibal pitched his camp on the plain between the hostile armies, and having concealed a portion of his troops among rough rocks, sent others to seize a neighbouring hillock, as a challenge to the foe. When Minucius had led out his forces to crush these, the men placed here and there in ambush by Hannibal suddenly sprang up, and would have annihilated Minucius's army, had not Fabius come to help them in their distress.100

23 When the same Hannibal was encamped in the depths of winter at the Trebia, with the camp of the consul, Sempronius Longus, in plain view and only the river flowing between, he placed Mago and picked men in ambush. Then he commanded Numidian cavalry to advance up to Sempronius's fortifications, in order to lure forth the simple-minded Roman. At the same time, he ordered these troops to retire by familiar fords at our first onset. By heedlessly attacking and pursuing the Numidians, the consul gave his troops a chill, as a result of fording the stream in the bitter cold and without breakfast. Then, when our men were suffering from numbness and hunger, Hannibal led against them his own troops, whom he had got in condition for that purpose by warm fires, food, and rubbing down with oil. Mago also did his part, and cut to pieces the rear of his enemy at the point where he had been posted for the purpose.101

24 At Trasimenus, where a narrow way,102 running out between the lake and the base of the hills, led out to the open plain, the same Hannibal, feigning flight, made his way through the narrow road to the open districts and pitched his camp there. Then, posting soldiers by night at various points over the rising ground of the hill and at the ends of the defile, at daybreak, under cover of a fog, he marshalled his line of battle. Flaminius, pursuing the enemy, who seemed to be retreating, entered the defile and did not see the ambush until he was surrounded in front, flank, and rear, and was annihilated with his army.103

25 The same Hannibal, when contending against the dictator Junius,104 ordered six hundred cavalrymen to break up into a number of squadrons, and at dead of night to appear in successive detachments without intermission around the camp of the enemy. Thus all night long the Romans were harassed and worn out by sentry duty on the rampart and by the rain, which happened to fall continuously, so that in the morning, when Junius gave the signal for recall, Hannibal led out his own troops, who had been well rested, and took Junius's camp by assault.105

26 In the same way, when the Spartans had draw entrenchments across the Isthmus and were defending the Peloponnesus, Epaminondas, the Theban, with the help of a few light-armed troops, harassed the enemy all night long. Then at daybreak, after he had recalled his own men and the Spartans had also retired, he suddenly moved forward the entire force which he had kept at rest, and burst directly through the ramparts, which had been left without defenders.106

27 At the battle of Cannae, Hannibal, having drawn up his line of battle, ordered six hundred Numidian cavalry to go over to the enemy. To prove their sincerity, these surrendered their swords and shields to our men, and were dispatched to the rear. Then, as soon as the engagement began, drawing out small swords, which they had secreted, and picking up the shield of the fallen, they slaughtered the troops of the Romans.107

28 Under pretence of surrender, the Iapydes handed over some of their to best men to Publius Licinius, the Roman proconsul. These were received and placed in the last line, whereupon they cut to pieces the Romans who were bringing up the rear.

29 Scipio Africanus, when facing the two hostile camps of Syphax and the Carthaginians, decided to make a night attack on that of Syphax, where there was a large supply of inflammable material, and to set fire to it, in order thus to cut down the Numidians as the army scurried in terror from their camp, and also, by laying ambuscades, to catch the Carthaginians, who, he knew, would rush forward to assist their allies. Both plans succeeded. For when the enemy rushed forward unarmed, thinking the conflagration accidental, Scipio fell upon them and cut them to pieces.108

30 Mithridates, after repeated defeats in battle at the hands of Lucullus, made an attempt against his life by treachery, hiring a certain Adathas, a man of extraordinary strength, to desert and to perpetrate the deed, so soon as he should gain the confidence of the enemy. This plan the deserter did his best to execute, but his efforts failed. For, though admitted by Lucullus to the cavalry troop, he was quietly kept under surveillance, since it was neither well to put trust at once in a deserter, nor to prevent other deserters from coming. After this fellow had exhibited a ready and earnest devotion on repeated raids, and had won confidence, he chose a time when the dismissal of the staff-officers brought with it repose throughout the camp, and caused the general's headquarters to be less frequented. Chance favoured Lucullus; for whereas the deserter expected to find Lucullus awake, in which case he would have been at once admitted to his presence, he actually found him at that time fast asleep, exhausted with revolving plans in his mind the night before. Then when Adathas pleaded to be admitted, on the ground that he had an unexpected and imperative message to deliver, he was kept out by the determined efforts of the slaves, who were concerned for their master's health. Fearing consequently that he was an object of suspicion, he mounted the horse which he held in readiness outside the gate, and fled to Mithridates without accomplishing his purpose.109

31 When Sertorius was encamped next to Pompey near the town of Lauron in Spain, there were only two tracts from which forage could be gathered, one nearby, the other farther off. Sertorius gave orders that the one nearby should be continually raided by light-armed troops, but that remoter one should not be visited by any troops. Thus, he finally convinced his adversaries that the more distant tract was safer. When, on one occasion, Pompey's troops had gone to this region, Sertorius ordered Octavius Graecinus, with ten cohorts armed after the Roman fashion, and ten cohorts of light-armed Spaniards along with Tarquinius Priscus and two thousand cavalry, set forth to lay an ambush against the foragers. These men executed their instructions with energy; for after examining the ground, they hid the above-mentioned forces by night in a neighbouring wood, posting the light-armed Spaniards in front, as best suited to stealthy warfare, the shield-bearing soldiers a little further back, and the cavalry in the rear, in order that the plan might not be betrayed by the neighing of the horses. Then they ordered all to repose in silence till the third hour of the following day.110 When Pompey's men, entertaining no suspicion and loaded down with forage, thought of returning, and those who had been on guard, lured on by the situation, were slipping away to forage, suddenly the Spaniards, darting out with the swiftness characteristic of their race, poured forth upon the stragglers, inflicted many wounds upon them, and put them to rout, to their great amazement. Then, before resistance to this first assault could be organised, the shield-bearing troops, bursting forth from the forest, overthrew and routed the Romans who were returning to the ranks, while the cavalry, dispatched after those in flight, followed them all the way back to the camp, cutting them to pieces. Provision was also made that no one should escape. For two hundred and fifty reserve horsemen, sent ahead for the purpose, found it a simple matter to race forward by short cuts, and then to turn back and meet those who had first fled, before they reached Pompey's camp. On learning of this, Pompey sent out a legion under Decimus Laelius to reinforce his men, whereupon the cavalry of the enemy, withdrawing to the right flank, pretended to give way, and then, passing round the legion, assaulted it from the rear, while those who had followed up the foragers attacked it from the front also. Thus the legion with its

commander was crushed between the two lines of the enemy. When Pompey led out his entire army to help the legion, Sertorius exhibited his forces drawn up on the hillside, and thus baulked Pompey's purpose. Thus, in addition to inflicting a twofold disaster, as a result of the same strategy, Sertorius forced Pompey to be the helpless witness of the destruction of his own troops. This was the first battle between Sertorius and Pompey. According to Livy, ten thousand men were lost in Pompey's army, along with the entire transport.111

32 Pompey, when warring in Spain, having first posted troops here and there to attack from ambush, by feigning fear, drew the enemy on in pursuit, till they reached the place of the ambuscade. Then when the opportune moment arrived, wheeling about, he slaughtered the foe in front and on both flanks, and likewise captured their general, Perperna.112

33 The same Pompey, in Armenia, when Mithridates was superior to him in the number and quality of his cavalry, stationed three thousand light-armed men and five hundred cavalry by night in a valley under cover of bushes lying between the two camps. Then at daybreak he sent forth his cavalry against the position of the enemy, planning that, as soon as the full force of the enemy, cavalry and infantry, became engaged in battle, the Romans should gradually fall back, still keeping ranks, until they should afford room to those who had been stationed for the purpose of attacking from the rear to arise and do so. When this design turned out successfully, those who had seemed to flee turned about, enabling Pompey to cut to pieces the enemy thus caught in panic between his two lines. Our infantry also, engaging in hand-to-hand encounter, stabbed the horses of the enemy. That battle destroyed the faith which the king had reposed in his cavalry.113

34 In the Slave War, Crassus fortified two camps close beside the camp of the enemy, near Mt. Cantenna. Then, one night, he moved his forces, leading them all out and posting them at the base of the mountain above mentioned, leaving his headquarters tent in the larger camp in order to deceive the enemy. Dividing the cavalry into two detachments, he directed Lucius Quintius to oppose Spartacus with one division and fool him with a mock encounter; with the other to lure to combat the Germans and Gauls, of the faction of Castus and Cannicus, and, by feigning flight, to draw them on to the spot where Crassus himself had drawn up his troops in battle array. When the barbarians followed, the cavalry fell back to the flanks, and suddenly the Roman force disclosed itself and rushed forward with a shout. In that battle Livy tells us that thirty-five thousand armed men, with their commanders, were slain; five Roman eagles and twenty-six standards were recaptured, along with much other booty, including five sets of rods and axes.114

35 Gaius Cassius, when fighting in Syria against the Parthians and their leader Osaces, exhibited only cavalry in front, but had posted infantry in hiding on rough ground in the rear. Then, when his cavalry fell back and retreated over familiar roads, he drew the army of the Parthians into the ambush prepared for them and cut them to pieces.115

36 Ventidius, keeping his own men in camp on pretence of fear, caused the Parthians and Labienus, who were elated with victorious successes, to come out for battle. Having lured them into an unfavourable situation, he attacked them by surprise and so overwhelmed them that the Parthians refused to follow Labienus and evacuated the province.116

37 The same Ventidius, having himself only a small force available for use against the Parthians under Pharnastanes, but observing that the confidence of the enemy was growing in consequence of their numbers, posted eighteen cohorts at the side of the camp in a hidden valley, with cavalry stationed behind the infantry. Then he sent a very small detachment against the enemy. When these by feigning flight had drawn the enemy in hot pursuit beyond

the place of ambush, the force at the side rose up, whereupon Ventidius drove the Parthians in precipitate flight and slaughtered them, Pharnastanes among them.117

38 On one occasion when the camps of Gaius Caesar and Afranius were pitched in opposite plains, it was the special ambition of each side to secure possession of the neighbouring hills — a task of extreme difficulty on account of the jagged rocks. In these circumstances, Caesar marshalled his army as though to march back again to Ilerda, a move supported by his deficiency of supplies. Then, within a short time, making a small detour, he suddenly started to seize the hills. The followers of Afranius, alarmed at sight of this, just as though their camp had been captured, started out themselves at top speed to gain the same hills. Caesar, having forecast this turn of affairs, fell upon Afranius's men, before they could form — partly with infantry, which he had sent ahead, partly with cavalry sent up in the rear.118

39 Antonius, near Forum Gallorum, having heard that the consul Pansa was approaching, met his army by means of ambuscades, set here and there in the woodland stretches along the Aemilian Way, thus routing his troops and inflicting on Pansa himself a wound from which he died in a few days.119

40 Juba, king in Africa at the time of the Civil War, by feigning a retirement, once roused unwarranted elation in the heart of Curio. Under the influence of this mistaken hope, Curio, pursuing Sabborras, the king's general, who, he thought, was in flight, came to open plains, where, surrounded by the cavalry of the Numidians, he lost his army and perished himself.120

41 Melanthus, the Athenian general, on one occasion came out for combat, in response to the challenge of the king of the enemy, Xanthus, the Boeotian. As soon as they stood face to face, Melanthus exclaimed: "Your conduct is unfair, Xanthus, and contrary to agreement. I am alone, but you have come out with a companion against me." When Xanthus wondered who was following him and looked behind, Melanthus dispatched him with a single stroke, as his head was turned away.121

42 Iphicrates, the Athenian, on one occasion in the Chersonesus, aware that Anaxibius, commander of the Spartans, was proceeding with his troops by land, disembarked a large force of men from his vessels and placed them in ambush, but directed his ships to sail in full view of the enemy, as though loaded with all his forces. When the Spartans were thus thrown off their guard and apprehended no danger, Iphicrates, attacking them by land from the rear as they marched along, crushed and routed them.122

43 The Liburnians on one occasion, when they had taken a position among some shallows, by allowing only their heads to appear above the surface of the water, caused the enemy to believe that water was deep. In this way a galley which followed them became stranded on the shoal, and was captured.

44 Alcibiades, commander of the Athenians at the Hellespont against Mindarus, leader of the Spartans, having a large army and numerous vessels, landed some of his soldiers by night, and hid part of his ships behind certain headlands. He himself, advancing with a few troops, so as to lure the enemy on in scorn of his small force, fled when pursued, until he finally drew the foe into the trap which had been laid. Then attacking the enemy in the rear, as he disembarked, he cut him to pieces with the aid of the troops which he had landed for this very purpose.123

45 The same Alcibiades, on one occasion, with about to engage in a naval combat, erected a number of masts on a headland, and commanded the men whom he left there to spread sails on

these as soon as they noticed that the engagement had begun. By this means he caused the enemy to retreat, since they imagined another fleet was coming to his assistance.

46 Memnon, the Rhodian, in a naval encounter, possessing a fleet of two hundred ships, and wishing to lure the vessels of the enemy out to battle, made arrangements for raising the masts of only a few of his ships, ordering these to proceed first. When the enemy from a distance saw the number of masts, and from that inferred the number of vessels, they offered battle, but were fallen upon by a larger number of ships and defeated.

47 Timotheus, leader of the Athenians, when about to engage in a naval encounter with the Spartans, as soon as the Spartan fleet came out arrayed in line of battle, sent ahead twenty of his swiftest vessels, to baulk the enemy in every way by various tactics. Then as soon as he observed that the enemy were growing less active in their manoeuvres, he moved forward and easily defeated them, since they were already worn out.124

VI. On Letting the Enemy Escape, lest, Brought to Bay, He Renew the Battle in Desperationa

1 When the Gauls, after the battle fought under Camillus's generalship, desired boats to cross the Tiber, the Senate voted to set them across and to supply them with provisions as well.

On a subsequent occasion also a free passage was afforded to the people of the same race when retreating through the Pomptine district. This road goes by the name of the "Gallic Way."125

2 Titus Marcius, a Roman knight, on whom the army conferred the supreme command after the two Scipios were slain, succeeded in enveloping the Carthaginians. When the latter, in order not to die unavenged, fought with increasing fury, Marcius opened up the maniples, afforded room for escape, and as the enemy became separated, slaughtered them without danger to his own men.126

3 When certain Germans whom Gaius Caesar had penned in fought the more fiercely from desperation, he ordered them to be allowed to escape, and then attacked them as they fled.

4 At Trasimenus, when the Romans had been enveloped and were fighting with the greatest fury, Hannibal opened up his ranks and gave them an opportunity of escape, whereupon, as they fled, he overwhelmed them without loss of his own troops.127

5 When the Aetolians, blockaded by Antigonus, king of the Macedonians, were suffering from famine and had resolved to make a sally in face of certain death, Antigonus afforded them an avenue of flight. Thus having cooled their ardour, he attacked them from the rear and cut them to pieces.128

6 Agesilaus, the Spartan, when engaged in battle with the Thebans, noticed that the enemy, hemmed in by the character of the terrain, were fighting with greater fury on account of their desperation. Accordingly he opened up his ranks and afforded the Thebans a way of escape. But when they tried to retreat, he again enveloped them, and cut them down from behind without loss of his own troops.129

p169 7 Gnaeus Manlius, the consul, on returning from battle found the camp of the Romans in possession of the Etruscans. He therefore posted guards at all the gates and roused the enemy, thus shut up within, to such a pitch of fury that he himself was slain in the fighting. When his lieutenants realized the situation, they withdrew the guards from one gate and afforded the Etruscans an opportunity of escape. But when the latter poured forth, the Romans pursued them and cut them to pieces, with the help of the other consul, Fabius, who happened to come up.130

8 When Xerxes had been defeated and the Athenians wished to destroy his bridge,131 Themistocles prevented this, showing that it was better for them that Xerxes should be expelled from Europe than be forced to fight in desperation. He also sent to the king a messenger to tell him in what danger he would be, in case he failed to make a hasty retreat.132

9 When Pyrrhus, king of the Epirotes, had captured a certain city and had noticed that the inhabitants, shut up inside, had closed the gates and were fighting valiantly from dire necessity, he gave them an opportunity to escape.

10 The same Pyrrhus, among many other precepts on the art of war, recommended never to press relentlessly on the heels of an enemy in flight — not merely in order to prevent the enemy from resisting too furiously in consequence of necessity, but also to make him more inclined to withdraw another time, knowing that the victor would not strive to destroy him when in flight.

VII. On Concealing Reverses

1 Tullus Hostilius, king of the Romans, on one occasion had engaged in battle with the Veientines, when the Albans, deserting the army of the Romans, made for the neighbouring hills. Since this action disconcerted our troops, Tullus shouted in a loud voice that the Albans had done that by his instructions, with the object of enveloping the foe. This declaration struck terror into the hearts of the Veientines and lent confidence to the Romans. By this device he turned the tide of battle.133

2 When a lieutenant of Lucius Sulla had gone over to the enemy at the beginning on an engagement, accompanied by a considerable force of cavalry, Sulla announced that this had been done by his own instructions. He thereby not merely saved his men from panic, but encouraged them by a certain expectation of advantage to result from this plan.

3 The same Sulla, when certain auxiliary troops dispatched by him had been surrounded and cut to pieces by the enemy, fearing that his entire army would be in a panic on account of this disaster, announced that he had purposely placed the auxiliaries in a place of danger, since they had plotted to desert. In this way he veiled a very palpable reverse under the guise of discipline, and encouraged his soldiers by convincing them that he had done this.

4 When the envoys of King Syphax told Scipio in the name of their king not to cross over to Africa from Sicily in expectation of an alliance, Scipio, fearing that the spirits of his men would receive a shock, if the hope of a foreign alliance were cut off, summarily dismissed the envoys, and spread abroad the report that he was expressly sent for by Syphax.134

5 Once when Quintus Sertorius was engaged in battle, he plunged a dagger into the barbarian who had reported to him that Hirtuleius had fallen, for fear the messenger might bring this news to the knowledge of others and in this way the spirit of his own troops should be broken.135

6 When Alcibiades, the Athenian, was hard pressed in battle by the Abydenes and suddenly noticed a courier approaching at great speed and with dejected countenance, he prevented the

courier from telling openly what tidings he brought. Having privately learned that his fleet was beset by Pharnabazus, the commander of the king, he concealed the fact both from the enemy and from his own soldiers, and finished the battle. Then straightway marching to rescue his fleet, he bore aid to his friends.136

7 When Hannibal entered Italy, three thousand Carpetani deserted him. Fearing that rest of his troops might be affected by their example, he proclaimed that they had been discharged by him, and as further proof of that, he sent home a few others whose services were of very little importance.137

8 When Lucius Lucullus noticed that the Macedonian cavalry, whom he had as auxiliaries, were suddenly deserting to the enemy in a body, he ordered the trumpets to sound and sent out squadrons to pursue the deserters. The enemy, thinking that an engagement was beginning, received the deserters with javelins, whereupon the Macedonians, seeing that they were not welcomed by the enemy and were attacked by those whom they were deserting, were forced to resort to a genuine battle and assaulted the enemy.138

9 Datames, commander of the Persians against Autophradates in Cappadocia, learning that part of his cavalry were deserting, ordered the rest of his troops to follow with him. Upon coming up with the deserters, he commended them for outstripping him in their eagerness, and also urged them to attack the enemy courageously. Seized with shame and penitence, the deserters changed their purpose, imagining that it had not been detected.139

10 The consul Titus Quinctius Capitolinus, when the Romans yielded ground in battle, falsely claimed that the enemy had been routed on the other flank. By thus lending courage to his men, he won a victory.140

11 When Marius was fighting against the Etruscans, his colleague Marcus Fabius, commander of the left flank, was wounded, and that section of the army therefore gave way, imagining that the consul had been slain. Thereupon Manlius confronted the broken line with squadrons of horse, shouting that his colleague was alive and that he himself had been victorious on the right flank. By this dauntless spirit, he restored the courage of his men and won the victory.141

12 When Marius was fighting against the Cimbrians and Teutons, his engineers on one occasion had heedlessly chosen such a site for the camp that the barbarians controlled the water supply. In response to the soldiers' demand for water, Marius pointed with his finger toward the enemy and said: "There is where you must get it." Thus inspired, the Romans straightway drove the barbarians from the place.142

13 Titus Labienus, after the Battle of Pharsalia, when his side had been defeated and he himself had fled to Dyrrhachium, combined falsehood with truth, and while not concealing the outcome of the battle, pretended that the fortunes of the two sides had been equalized in consequence of a severe wound received by Caesar. By this pretence, he created confidence in the other followers of Pompey's party.143

14 Marcus Cato, having inadvertently landed with a single galley in Ambracia at a time when the allied fleet was blockaded by the Aetolians, although he had no troops with him, began nevertheless to make signals by voice and gesture, in order to give the impression that he was summoning the approaching ships of his own forces. By this earnestness he alarmed the enemy, just as though the troops, whom he pretended to be summoning from near at hand,

were visibly approaching. The Aetolians, accordingly, fearing that they would be crushed by the arrival of the Roman fleet, abandoned the blockade.144

VIII. On Restoring Morale by Firmness

1 In the battle in which King Tarquinius encountered the Sabines, Servius Tullius, then a young man, noticing that the standard-bearers fought halfheartedly, seized a standard and hurled it into the ranks of the enemy. To recover it, the Romans fought so furiously that they not only regained the standard, but also won the day.145

2 The consul Furius Agrippa, when on one occasion his flank gave way, snatched a military standard from a standard-bearer and hurled it into the hostile ranks of the Hernici and Aequi. By this act the day was saved, for the Romans with the greatest eagerness pressed forward to recapture the standard.146

3 The consul Titus Quinctius Capitolinus hurled a standard into the midst of the hostile ranks of the Faliscans and commanded his troops to regain it.147

4 Marcus Furius Camillus, military tribune with consular power, on one occasion when his troops held back, seized a standard-bearer by the hand and dragged him into the hostile ranks of the Volscians and Latins, whereupon the rest were shamed into following.148

5 Salvius, the Pelignian, did the same in the Persian War.149

6 Marcus Furius, meeting his army in retreat, declared he would receive in camp no one who was not victorious. Thereupon he led them back to battle and won the day.150

7 Scipio, at Numantia, seeing his forces in retreat, proclaimed that he would treat as an enemy whoever should return to camp.151

8 The dictator Servilius Priscus, having given the command to carry the standards of the legions against the hostile Faliscans, ordered the standard-bearer to be executed for hesitating to obey. The rest, cowed by this example, advanced against the foe.152

9 Cornelius Cossus, master of the horse, did the same in an engagement with the people of Fidenae.153

10 Tarquinius, when his cavalry showed hesitation in the battle against the Sabines, ordered them to fling away their bridles, put spurs to their horses, and break through the enemy's line.

11 In the Samnite War, the consul Marcus Atilius, seeing his troops quitting the battle and taking refuge in camp, met them with his own command and declared that they would have to fight against him and all loyal citizens, unless they preferred to fight against the enemy. In this way he marched them back in a body to the battle.154

12 When Sulla's legions broke before the hosts of Mithridates led by Archelaus, Sulla advanced with drawn sword into the first line and, addressing his troops, told them, in case anybody asked where they had left their general, to answer: "Fighting in Boeotia." Shamed by these words, they followed him to a man.155

13 The deified Julius, when his troops gave way at Munda, ordered his horse to be removed from sight, and strode forward as a foot-soldier to the front line. His men, ashamed to desert their commander, thereupon renewed the fight.156

14 Philip, on one occasion, fearing that his troops would not withstand the onset of the Scythians, stationed the trustiest of his cavalry in the rear, and commanded them to permit no one of their comrades to quit the battle, but to kill them if they persisted in retreating. This proclamation induced even the most timid to prefer to be killed by the enemy rather than by their own comrades, and enabled Philip to win the day.157

On Measures taken after Battle

IX. On Bringing the War to a Close after a Successful Engagement

1 After Gaius Marius had defeated the Teutons in battle, and night had put an end to the conflict, he encamped round about the remnants of his opponents. By causing a small group of his own men to raise loud cries from time to time, he kept the enemy in a state of alarm and prevented them from securing rest. He thus succeeded more easily in crushing them on the following day, since they had had no sleep.158

2 Claudius Nero, having met the Carthaginians on their way from Spain to Italy under the command of Hasdrubal, defeated them and threw Hasdrubal's head into Hannibal's camp. As a result, Hannibal was overwhelmed with grief and the army gave up hope of receiving reinforcements.159

3 When Lucius Sulla was besieging Praeneste, he fastened on spears the heads of Praenestine generals who had been slain in battle, and exhibited them to the besieged inhabitants, thus breaking their stubborn resistance.160

4 Arminius, leader of the Germans, likewise fastened on spears the heads of those he had slain, and ordered them to be brought up to the fortifications of the enemy.161

5 When Domitius Corbulo was besieging Tigranocerta and the Armenians seemed likely to make an obstinate defence, Corbulo executed Vadandus, one of the nobles he had captured, shot his head out of a balista, and sent it flying within the fortifications of the enemy. It happened to fall in the midst of a council which the barbarians were holding at that very moment, and the sight of it (as though it were some portent) so filled them with consternation that they made haste to surrender.162

6 When Hermocrates, the Syracusan, had defeated the Carthaginians in battle, and was afraid that the prisoners, of whom he had taken an enormous number, would be carelessly guarded, since the successful issue of the struggle might prompt the victors to revelry and neglect, he pretended that the cavalry of the enemy were planning an attack on the following night. By instilling this fear, he succeeded in having the guard over the prisoners maintained even more carefully than usual.

7 When the same Hermocrates had achieved certain successes, and for that reason his men, through a spirit of over-confidence, had abandoned all restraint and were sunk in a drunken stupor, he sent a deserter into the camp of the enemy to prevent their flight by declaring that ambuscades of Syracusans had been posted everywhere. From fear of these, the enemy

remained in camp. Having thus detained them, Hermocrates, on the following day, when his own men were more fit, gave the enemy over to their mercy and ended the war.163

8 When Miltiades had defeated a huge host of Persians at Marathon, and the Athenians were losing time in rejoicing over the victory, he forced them to hurry to bear aid to the city, at which the Persian fleet was aiming. Having thus got ahead of the enemy, he filled the walls with warriors, so that the Persians, thinking that the number of the Athenians was enormous and that they themselves had met one army at Marathon while another was now confronting them on the walls, straightway turned their vessels about and laid their course for Asia.164

9 When the fleet of the Megarians approached Eleusis at night with the object of kidnapping the Athenian matrons who had made sacrifice to Ceres, Pisistratus, the Athenian, engaged it in battle and, by ruthlessly slaughtering the enemy, avenged his own countrymen. Then he filled these same captured ships with Athenian soldiers, placing in full view certain matrons dressed as captives. The Megarians, deceived by these appearances, thinking their own people were sailing back, and that, too, crowned with victory, rushed out to meet them, in disorder and without weapons, whereupon they were a second time overwhelmed.165

10 Cimon, the Athenian general, having defeated the fleet of the Persians near the island of Cyprus, fitted out his men with the weapons of the prisoners and in the barbarians' own ships set sail to meet the enemy in Pamphylia, near the Eurymedon River. The Persians, recognizing the vessels and the garb of those standing on deck, were quite off their guard. Thus on the same day they were suddenly crushed in two battles, one on sea and one on land.166

X. On Repairing One's Losses after a Reverse

1 When Titus Didius was warring in Spain and had fought an extremely bitter engagement, to which darkness put an end, leaving a large number of slain on both sides, he provided for the burial by night of many bodies of his own men. On the following day, the Spaniards, coming out to perform a like duty, found more of their men slain than of the Romans, and arguing according to this calculation that they had been beaten, came to terms with the Roman commander.167

2 Titus Marcius, a Roman knight, who had charge of the remnants of the army [of the Scipios] in Spain, seeing near at hand two camps of the Carthaginians a few miles distant from each other, urged on his men and attacked the nearer camp at dead of night. Since the enemy, being flushed with victory, were without organization, Marcius by his attack did not leave so much as a single man to report the disaster. Granting his troops merely the briefest time for rest, and outstripping the news of his exploit, he attacked the second camp the same night. Thus, by a double success, he destroyed the Carthaginians in both places and restored to the Roman people the lost provinces of Spain.168

XI. On Ensuring the Loyalty of Those Whom One Mistrusts

1 When Publius Valerius had an insufficient garrison at Epidaurus and therefore feared perfidy on the part of the townspeople, he prepared to celebrate athletic contests at some distance from the city. When nearly all the population had gone there to see the show, he closed the gates and refused to admit the Epidaurians until he had taken hostages from their chief men.

2 Gnaeus Pompey, suspecting the Chaucensians and fearing that they would not admit a garrison, asked that they would meanwhile permit his invalid soldiers to recover among them. Then, sending his strongest men in the guise of invalids, he seized the city and held it.

3 When Alexander had conquered and subdued Thrace and was setting out for Asia, fearing that after his departure the Thracians would take up arms, he took with him, as though by way of conferring honour, their kings and officials — all in fact who seemed to take to heart the loss of freedom. In charge of those left behind he placed common and ordinary persons, thus preventing the officials from wishing to make any change, as being bound to him by favours, and the common people from even being able to do so, since they had been deprived of their leaders.169

4 When Antipater beheld the army of the Peloponnesians, who had assembled to assail his authority on hearing of the death of Alexander, he pretended not to understand with what purpose they had come, and thanked them for having gathered to aid Alexander against the Spartans adding that he would write to the king about this.170 But inasmuch as he did not need their assistance at present, he urged them to go home, and by this statement dispelled the danger which threatened him from the now order of affairs.171

5 When Scipio Africanus was warring in Spain, there was brought before him among the captive women a noble maiden of surpassing beauty who attracted the gaze of everyone. Scipio guarded her with the greatest pains and restored her to her betrothed, Alicius by name, presenting to him likewise, as a marriage gift, the gold which her parents had brought to Scipio as a ransom. Overcome by this manifold generosity, the whole tribe leagued itself with the government of Rome.172

6 The story goes that Alexander of Macedon likewise, having taken captive a maiden of exceeding beauty betrothed to the chief of a neighbouring tribe, treated her with such extreme consideration that he refrained even from gazing at her. When the maiden was later returned to her lover, Alexander, as a result of this kindness, secured the attachment of the entire tribe.173

7 When the Emperor Caesar Augustus Germanicus,174 in the war in which he earned his title by conquering the Germans, was building forts in the territory of the Cubii, he ordered compensation to be made for the crops which he had included within his fortifications. Thus the renown of his justice won the allegiance of all.175

XII. What to do for the Defence of the Camp, in case a Commander lacks Confidence in his Present Forces

1 The consul, Titus Quinctius, as the Volscians were about to attack his camp, kept only one cohort on duty, and dismissed the remainder of the army to take their rest, directing the trumpeters to mount their horses and make the round of the camp sounding their trumpets. By exhibiting this semblance of strength, he kept the enemy off and held them throughout the night. Then at daybreak, attacking them by a sudden sortie when they were exhausted with watching, he easily defeated them.176

2 Quintus Sertorius, when in Spain, was completely outmatched by the cavalry of the enemy, who in their excessive confidence advanced up to his very fortifications. Accordingly during the night he constructed trenches and drew up his line of battle in front of them. Then when the cavalry approached, as was their wont, he drew back his line. The enemy following close on his heels, fell into the trenches and thus were defeated.177

3 Chares, the Athenian commander, on one occasion was expecting reinforcements, but feared that meanwhile the enemy, despising his small force, would attack his camp. He therefore ordered that a number of the soldiers under his command should pass out at night by the rear of the camp, and should return by a route where they would be clearly observed by the enemy,

thus creating the impression that fresh forces were arriving. In this way, he defended himself by pretended reinforcements, until he was equipped with those he was expecting.178

4 Iphicrates, the Athenian, being encamped on one occasion on level ground, happened to learn that the Thracians were intending to come down from the hills, over which there was but a single line of descent, with the purpose of plundering his camp by night. He therefore secretly led forth his troops and posted them on both sides of the road over which the Thracians were to pass. Then when the enemy descended upon the camp, in which a large number of watch-fires, built by the hands of a few men, produced the impression that a mighty host was still there, Iphicrates was enabled to attack them on the flank and crush them.179

XIII. On Retreating

1 When the Gauls were about to fight with Attalus, they handed over all their gold and silver to trusty guards, with instructions to scatter, in case their p197forces should be routed in battle, in order that thereby the enemy might be occupied in picking up the spoils and they themselves might more easily escape.180

2 Tryphon, king of Syria, when defeated, scattered money along the whole line of his retreat. While the cavalry of Antiochus delayed to pick this up, he effected his escape.181

3 Quintus Sertorius, when defeated in battle by Quintus Metellus Pius, being convinced that not even an organized retreat was safe, commanded his soldiers to disband and retire, informing them at what point he desired them to reassemble.182

4 Viriathus, leader of the Lusitanians, extricated himself from an awkward position, and from the menace of our troops, by the same method as Sertorius, disbanding his forces and then reassembling.183

5 Horatius Cocles, when Porsenna's army was pressing hard upon him, commanded his supporters to return over the bridge to the City, and then to destroy the bridge in order that the foe might not follow them. While this was being done, he himself, as defender of the bridgehead, held up the oncoming enemy. Then, when the crash told him that the bridge had been destroyed, he threw himself into the stream, and swam across it in his armour, exhausted though he was by wounds.184

6 Afranius, when fleeing from Caesar near Ilerda in Spain, pitched camp, while Caesar was pressing close upon him. When Caesar did the same and sent his men off to gather forage, Afranius suddenly gave the signal to continue the retreat.185

7 When Anthony was retreating, hard pressed by the Parthians, as often as he broke camp at daybreak, his retiring troops were assailed by volleys of arrows from the barbarians. Accordingly one day he kept his men back till nearly noon, thus producing the impression that he had made a permanent camp. As soon as the Parthians had become persuaded of this and had withdrawn, he accomplished his regular march for the remainder of the day without interference.186

8 When Philip had suffered defeat in Epirus, in order that the Romans might not overwhelm him in flight, he secured the grant of a truce to bury the dead. In consequence of this, the guards relaxed their vigilance, so that Philip slipped away.187

9 Publius Claudius, defeated by the Carthaginians in a naval engagement and thinking it necessary to break through the forces of the enemy, ordered his twenty remaining vessels to be dressed out as though victorious. The Carthaginians, therefore, thought our men had proved themselves superior in the encounter, so that Claudius became an object of fear to the enemy and thus made his escape.188

10 The Carthaginians, on one occasion, when defeated in a naval battle, desiring to shake off the Romans who were close upon them, pretended that their vessels had caught on shoals and imitated the movement of stranded galleys. In this way they caused the victors, in fear of meeting a like disaster, to afford them an opportunity of escape.

11 Commius, the Atrebatian, when defeated by the deified Julius, fled from Gaul to Britain, and happened to reach the Channel at a time when the wind was fair, but the tide was out. Although the vessels were stranded on the flats, he nevertheless ordered the sails to be spread. Caesar, who was following them from a distance, seeing the sails swelling with the full breeze, and imagining Commius to be escaping from his hands and to be proceeding on a prosperous voyage, abandoned the pursuit.

The Editor's Notes:

1 Scipio's troops have lunch: 206 B.C. Cf. Polyaen. VIII.XVI.1.

2 Metellus' noonday attack: 76 B.C.

3 Postumius wears the enemy down: 262 B.C.

4 Iphicrates attacks at lunchtime: Cf. Polyaen. III.IX.53.

5 Iphicrates uses non-combatants as a supply force: 393-392 B.C. Cf. Polyaen. III.IX.52.

6 Verginius' breathless enemies: 494 B.C. Cf. Livy II.XXX.10 ff.

7 Fabius Maximus wears down the Gauls and Samnites: 295 B.C. Cf. Livy X.28 ff.

8 Philip draws out an engagement: 338 B.C. Cf. Polyaen. IV.II.7; Justin. IX.III.9.

9 their troops had slain all their beasts of burden: The motive was to be less encumbered on the march.

10 Caesar's desperate opponents: 49 B.C. Cf. Caes. B.C. I.81 ff.

11 Pompey's night-time encounter: 66 B.C. Cf. Flor. III.V.22-24; Plut. Pomp. 32 ff.

12 Jugurtha's battles late in the day: 111-106 B.C. Cf. Sall. Jug. XCVIII.2.

13 Lucullus attacks the Armenians before they're ready: 69 B.C. Cf. Plut. Lucul. 26-28; Appian Mithr. 84-85.

14 Tiberius Nero delays battle: 12-10 B.C. or 6-9 A.D. The future Emperor Tiberius.

15 Caesar takes advantage of the enemy's superstition: 58 B.C. Cf. Caes. B. G. I.50; Plut. Caes. 19.

16 Vespasian and the sabbath of the Jews: 70 A.D.

17 Lysander's regular attacks: 405 B.C. Cf. Xen. Hell. II.I.21 ff.; Plut. Lysand. 10-11.

18 Manius Curius fights in confined quarters: 281-275 B.C.

19 Pompey bears down on the enemy from a height: 66 B.C.

20 Caesar fires his artillery at the enemy from a height: 47 B.C. Cf. Bell. Alexandr. 73-76.

21 Lucullus bears down on the enemy from a height: 69 B.C. Cf. Plut. Lucul. 28; Appian Mithr. 85.

22 Ventidius — "don't fire till you see the whites of their eyes": 38 B.C. Cf. Flor. IV.IX.6.

23 Hannibal protects his flanks by hollows and precipitous roads: 210 B.C. According to Livy XXVII.II.4 and Plut. Marc. 24, the result of the battle was indecisive.

24 Hannibal's enemies have sand in their eyes: 216 B.C. Cf. Val. Max. VII.IV.ext.2; Plut. Fab. 16; Livy XXII.43, 46. In none of these accounts is a river mentioned as the source of the wind. Livy speaks of the ventus Volturnus.

25 Marius tires out his enemies then puts the sun and wind and dust in their eyes: 101 B.C. Cf. Plut. Mar. 26; Polyaen. VIII.X.3.

26 Cleomenes' prepared battlefield: 510 B.C.

27 Xanthippus chooses to fight in the plain: 255 B.C. Cf. Polyb. I.33 ff.; Zonar. VIII.13.

28 Epaminondas raises some dust: 362 B.C. Cf. Polyaen. II.III.14.

29 the Spartans even the odds in the pass of Thermopylae: 480 B.C. Cf. Herod. VII.201 ff.; Polyaen. VII.XV.5.

30 Themistocles turns "traitor" and keeps the enemy awake: 480 B.C. Cf. Herod. VIII.75; Plut. Them. 12; Nep. Them. 4.

31 Scipio attacks the weakest forces: 218 B.C. Cn. Cornelius Scipio Calvus. Cf. Polyb. III.76.

32 Hyllians: Illyrians.

33 Philip attacks the weakest forces: 359 B.C. Cf. Diodor. XVI.4.

34 Pammenes draws away his strongest opponents: 353 B.C. Cf. Polyaen. V.XVI.2.

35 Scipio changes his formation: 206 B.C. Cf. Livy XXVIII.14-15; Polyb. XI.22 ff.

36 Metellus nullifies his opponents' strongest forces: 76 B.C. Q. Caecilius Metellus Pius.

37 Artaxerxes' slow centre: 401 B.C. Battle of Cunaxa. Cf. Xen. Anab. I.VIII.10.

38 Hannibal's precision use of his army: 216 B.C. Cf. Livy XXII.47; Polyb. III.115.

39 Xanthippus reserves his best troops: 207 B.C. Battle of the Metaurus. Cf. Livy XXVII.48.

40 auxiliary troops: These were the "light-armed troops," already mentioned.

41 Xanthippus' use of his troops: 255 B.C.

42 Sertorius reserves his best troops: Cf. II.V.31.

43 Cleandridas' close-order formation: After 443 B.C. Cf. Polyaen. II.X.4.

44 Gastron's troop switch: Cf. Polyaen. II.16.

45 Pompey's concealed infantry: 65 B.C. Cf. Dio XXXVII.4.

46 testudo: In the testudo, the soldiers secured protection by holding their over-lapped shields above their heads, a formation whose appearance suggested the scales of a tortoise.

47 Mark Antony's testudo: 36 B.C. Cf. Dio XLIX.29-30; Plut. Anton. 45.

48 hastati, principes, and triarii: These names designate three successive lines of battle. The hastati were the first line; the two other lines were drawn up behind these.

49 Scipio's flexible use of the standard Roman battle formation: 202 B.C. Battle of Zama. Cf. Livy XXX.33, 35; Polyb. XV.IX.6-10, XV.XI.1-3; Appian Pun. 40-41. Livy and Polybius put Laelius on the left wing and Masinissa on the right; Appian puts Laelius on the right and Octavius on the left.

50 postsignani: Troops posted behind the standards.

51 antesignani: Troops posted in front of the standards and serving for their defence.

52 Sulla against Archelaus: 86 B.C.

53 Alexander's army facing in all directions: 331 B.C. Cf. Curt. IV.XIII.30-32; Diodor. XVII.LVII.5.

54 Paulus uses up the enemy's spears: 168 B.C. Battle of Pydna. Cf. Livy XLIV.41; Plut. Aem. 20.

55 the Homeric verse: Iliad IV.299 seems to have become proverbial; cf. Ammian. Marc. XXIV.VI.9.

56 The Romans' judicious use of different kinds of troops: 279 B.C. Cf. Plut. Pyrrh. 21.

57 Old Pharsalus: A town in Thessaly near Pharsalus.

58 foot-soldiers trained in cavalry fighting: i.e. in fighting in conjunction with cavalry — doubtless after the method detailed in Caesar's Gallic War, I.48.

59 Caesar's reserves: 48 B.C. Cf. Caes. B.C. III.89, 93, 94; Plut. Caes. 44, Pomp. 69.

60 The Emperor Caesar Augustus Germanicus: Domitian.

61 Domitian commands his cavalry to fight on foot: 83 A.D. Cf. Suet. Domit. 6.

62 Duilius' grappling-hook: 260 B.C. Cf. Flor. II.I.8-9; Polyb. I.22.

63 Papirius Cursor, the son: Of the dictator.

64 Papirius Cursor's colleague: Spurius Carvilius.

65 Papirius Cursor's phantom reinforcements: 293 B.C. Cf. Livy X.40-41.

66 hastati: First-line troops.

67 Fabius Maximus' use of a hill: 297 B.C. Cf. Livy X.14.

68 Minucius Rufus' phantom multitude: 109 B.C.

69 Porcius Cato appears in the enemy's rear: 191 B.C. Cf. Livy XXXVI.14-19; Plut. Cat. Maj. 12 ff.; Appian Syr. 17 ff.

70 Sulpicius Peticus' phantom reinforcements: 358 B.C. Peticus was dictator in this year, having been consul in 364 and 361. Cf. Livy VII.14-15. Appian Gall. 1 gives a different stratagem.

71 Marius' phantom large cavalry unit: 102 B.C. Cf. Plut. Mar. 20; Polyaen. VIII.X.2.

72 Licinius Crassus sends a small force around the enemy's rear: 71 B.C.

73 Marcus Marcellus' loud battle-cry: 216 B.C. Cf. Livy XXIII.XVI.13-14.

74 Valerius Laevinus' bloody sword: 280 B.C. Cf. Plut. Pyrrh. 17.

75 Jugurtha's disinformation: 107 B.C. Cf. Sall. Jug. ci.6-8.

76 Myronides' victory: 457 B.C. Cf. Polyaen. I.XXXV.1.

77 Croesus' camels: 546 B.C. Cf.Herod. I.80; Polyaen. VII.VI.6; they attribute this stratagem to Cyrus.

78 Pyrrhus' elephants: 280 B.C. Cf. Flor. I.XVIII.8; Plut. Pyrrh. 17.

79 the Carthaginian elephants: Cf. II.V.4.

80 incendiary cattle: 229 B.C. Cf. Appian Hisp. 5.

81 The Faliscan and Tarquinian Furies: 356 B.C. Cf. Livy VII.XVII.3.

82 The Veientine and Fidenate Furies: 426 B.C. Cf. Livy IV.33; Flor. I.XII.7.

83 Atheas' phantom reinforcements: Cf. Polyaen. VII.XLIV.1.

84 Romulus' ambush at Fidenae: Cf. Livy I.14; Polyaen. VIII.III.2.

85 Fabius Maximus' ambush at Sutri: 310 B.C. Q. Fabius Maximus Rullianus. Cf. Livy IX.35.

86 Gracchus lures the enemy out: 179 B.C. Cf. Livy XL.48.

87 Panormus: The modern Palermo.

88 Lucius Metellus baits the Carthaginian elephants: 251 B.C. Cf. Polyb. I.40.

89 Thamyris' ambush: 529 B.C. Cf. Justin. I.8; Herod. I.204 ff.

90 Viriathus lures the enemy into bad terrain: 147-139 B.C. In II.XIII.4, Viriathus is dux Lusitanorum.

91 Fulvius deceives the enemy into betraying themselves: Livy XL.30-32 says that Q. Fulvius Flaccus used this stratagem with the Celtiberians in 181 B.C. There is no account of Fulvius's warring with the Cimbrians.

92 Leptines lays waste his own land: 397-396 B.C. Cf. Polyaen. V.VIII.1.

93 Maharbal: A Carthaginian officer under Hannibal.

94 Maharbal poisons the water: Polyaen. V.X.1 attributes this stratagem to Himilco, 396 B.C.

95 Tiberius Gracchus gives the enemy something to chew on: 179-178 B.C.

96 Alexander's phantom army: 327 B.C. Polyaen. IV.III.29 and Curt. VII.XI.1 tell of the employment of a different stratagem.

97 Memnon's deserters: Polyaen. V.XLIV.2 has a slightly different version.

98 Labienus' departure: 53 B.C. Cf. Caes. B. G. VI.7-8; Dio XL.31.

99 Hannibal lures the enemy on: 210 B.C. At Herdonia. Cf. Livy XXVII.1; Appian Hann. 48.

100 Hannibal capitalizes on the enemy's internal divisions: 217 B.C. Cf. Livy XXII.28; Polyb. III.104-105.

101 Hannibal's cold-water ambush: 218 B.C. Cf. Livy XXI.54 ff.; Polyb. III.71.

102 a narrow way at Trasimenus: Generally considered to be the narrow passage between the lake and Monte Gualandro, near Borghetto. Livy's description suits this locality; that of Polybius does not.

103 Hannibal ambushes the Romans at Lake Trasimenus: 217 B.C. Cf. Livy XXII.4; Polyb. III.83 ff.

104 the dictator Junius: M. Junius Pera.

105 Hannibal wears out the enemy: 216 B.C. At Capua. Cf. Polyaen. VI.XXXVIII.6; Zonar. IX.3.

106 Epaminondas wears out the enemy: 369 B.C. Cf. Polyaen. II.III.9.

107 Hannibal's Numidian cavalry infiltrators: 216 B.C. Cf. Livy XXII.48; Val. Max. VII.IV.ext.2; Appian Hann. 20 ff. Livy and Appian give the number as five hundred.

108 Scipio Africanus's fires: 203 B.C. Cf. Livy XXX.5-6; Polyb. XIV.4.

109 Mithridates's foiled attempt at assassination: 72 B.C. Cf. Appian Mithr. 79; Plut. Lucull. 16. The name of the deserter varies in the different accounts.

110 the third hour: About 9 A.M.

111 battle of Lauron: 76 B.C. Cf. Plut. Sert. 18; Appian B.C. I.109. The allusion to Livy cannot be identified.

112 Pompey's ambush in Spain: 72 B.C. Cf. Livy Per. 96; Oros. V.XXIII.13; Appian B.C. I.115.

113 Pompey's ambush in Armenia: 66 B.C. Cf. Appian Mithr. 98; Dio XXXVI.XLVII.3-4.

114 Crassus in the Slave War — a feint and an ambush: 71 B.C. Cf. Livy Per. 97; Plut. Crass. 11; Oros. V.XXIV.6.

115 Cassius' ambush in Syria: 51 B.C. Cf. Dio XL.29.

116 Ventidius' surprise attack: 39 B.C.Cf. Dio XLVIII.39-40; Justin. XLII.IV.7-8.

117 Ventidius ambushes the Parthians: 39 B.C. Cf. Dio XLVIII.XLI.1-4; Plut. Ant. 33.

118 Caesar feigned attack on a hill: 49 B.C. Cf. Caes. B.C. I.65-72.

119 Antonius ambushes Pansa: 43 B.C. Mutina. Cf. Appian B.C. III.66 ff.; Cic. ad Fam. X.30.

120 Juba's false retreat: 49 B.C. Cf. Caes. B.C. II.40-42; Dio XLI.41-42; Appian B.C. II.45.

121 Melanthus, "Whozat behind you?": Cf. Polyaen. I.19.

122 Iphicrates' nearly empty ships: 389-388 B.C. Cf. Xen. Hell. IV.VIII.32 ff.

123 Alcibiades' amphibian ambush: 410 B.C. Cf. Xen. Hell. I.I.11 ff.; Polyaen. I.XL.9; Diodor. XIII.50.

124 Timotheus wears the enemy down: 375 B.C. Cf. Polyaen. III.X.6, 12, 16.

125 the Romans let the Gauls go: 349 B.C. L. Furius Camillus, son of the great Camillus.

126 Titus Marcius lets the enemy escape, sort of: 212 B.C. Livy XXV.37 gives his praenomen as Lucius.

127 Hannibal lets the enemy escape, sort of: 217 B.C.

128 Antigonus lets the enemy escape, sort of: 223-221 B.C. Antigonus Doson.

129 Agesilaus lets the enemy escape, sort of: 394 B.C. Cf. Polyaen. II.I.19; Plut. Agesil. 18. Xen. Hell. IV.3 notes the failure of Agesilaus to employ this stratagem.

130 Gnaeus Manlius' lieutenants let the enemy escape, sort of: 480 B.C. Cf. Livy II.47.

131 Xerxes' bridge: i.e. the bridge which Xerxes had constructed across the Hellespont at the time of his invasion of Greece.

132 Themistocles lets Xerxes flee: 480 B.C. Cf. Justin. II.XIII.5 ff.; Polyaen. I.XXX.4. Plut. Them. 16 and Herod. VIII.108 attribute the advice against destroying the bridge to Aristides and Eurybiades respectively.

133 Tullus Hostilius masks a desertion: Cf. Livy I.27; Val. Max. VII.IV.1; Dionys. III.24. Nep. Ages. 6 and Datam. 6 attributes like stratagems to Agesilaus and Datames.

134 Scipio simulates an alliance: 204 B.C. Cf. Livy XXIX.23-24; Polyaen. VIII.XVI.7.

135 Sertorius enforces silence: 75 B.C.

136 Alcibiades keeps quiet: 409 B.C.

137 Hannibal masks a desertion: 218 B.C. Cf. Livy XXI.23.

138 Lucullus converts a desertion into a cavalry charge: 74-66 B.C.

139 Datames averts a desertion: 362 B.C. Nep. Datam. 6, Diodor. XV.91 and Polyaen. VII.XXI.7 give a slightly different version of this episode.

140 Capitolinus' disinformation: 468 B.C. Cf. Livy II.LXIV.5-7; Dionys. IX.57.

141 Marius gets the news out: 480 B.C. According to Livy II.46-47 and Dionys. IX.11, Q. Fabius and Manlius were wounded, and Marcus Fabius was the author of this stratagem.

142 Marius' source of water: 102 B.C. Cf. Flor. III.III.7-10; Plut. Mar. 18.

143 Labienus' disinformation: 48 B.C.

144 Cato's signals: 191 B.C.

145 Tarquin throws a standard into the ranks of the enemy: This type of stratagem was very frequently resorted to. Cf. Florus I.11; Val. Max. III.II.20; Caes. B. G. 4.25; Livy IV.XXIX.3 and passim.

146 Furius Agrippa throws a standard into the ranks of the enemy: 446 B.C. Cf. Livy III.LXX.2-11.

147 Titus Quinctius Capitolinus throws a standard into the ranks of the enemy: There is no other record of Titus Quinctius Capitolinus's warring with the Faliscans. Livy IV.29 attributes this stratagem to Titus Quinctius Cincinnatus in the war with the Volscians, 431 B.C.

148 Camillus throws a standard-bearer into the ranks of the enemy: 386 B.C. Cf. Livy VI.7-8.

149 Salvius throws a standard-bearer into the ranks of the enemy: Plut. Aem. 20 attributes to Salvius a stratagem similar to the first three of this chapter. 168 B.C.

150 Marcus Furius meets his army in retreat: 381 B.C. Camillus. Cf. Livy VI.24.

151 Scipio sees his forces retreating: 133 B.C.

152 Servilius Priscus executes a standard-bearer: 418 B.C. According to Livy IV.46-47, the battle was with the Aequi, not the Faliscans.

153 Cornelius Cossus executes a standard-bearer: 426 B.C. Cf. Livy IV.XXXIII.7; Flor. I.XI.2-3. This stratagem is similar to number 10, rather than number 8.

154 Marcus Atilius, "You're going to have to fight me": 294 B.C. Cf. Livy X.36. A slightly different version of this story is told in IV.I.29.

155 Whether his army comes along or not, Sulla fights in Boeotia: 85 B.C. Cf. Plut. Sulla 21; Polyaen. VIII.IX.2; Appian Mithr. 49.

156 Caesar fights on foot: 45 B.C. Cf. Plut. Caes. 56; Polyaen. VIII.XXIII.16; Vell. II.55.

157 Philip orders his troops to kill anyone who retreats: Justin. I.VI.10-13 attributes a similar stratagem to Astyages.

158 Marius makes noise at night: 102 B.C.

159 Claudius Nero uses Hasdrubal's head as a projectile: 207 B.C. Cf. Livy XXVII.51; Zonar. IX.9.

160 Sulla's heads: 82 B.C. Cf. Appian B.C. I.93-94.

161 Arminius's heads: 9 A.D.

162 Corbulo uses Vadandus' head as a projectile: 60 A.D.

163 Hermocrates buys rest for his men by a ruse: 413 B.C. Cf. Polyaen. I.XLIII.2; Thuc. VII.73; Plut. Nic. 26.

164 Miltiades doubles his army: 490 B.C. Cf. Herod. VI.115 ff.

165 Pisistratus' disguise: 604 B.C. Cf. Justin. II.8; Polyaen. I.XX.2; Plut. Solon 8.

166 Cimon's disguise: 466 B.C. Cf. Thuc. I.100; Polyaen. I.XXXIV.1; Diodor. XI.61.

167 Titus Didius' night burials: 98-93 B.C.

168 Titus Marcius attacks twice: 212 B.C. Livy XXV.37 gives his praenomen as Lucius.

169 Alexander deports the top ranks of an enemy population: 334 B.C. Cf. Justin. XI.V.1-3.

170 Antipater says thank you. . .: i.e. he intentionally acted on the assumption that they had not heard of the death of Alexander, though he knew this assumption to be false.

171 . . . and dispels danger: 331-330 B.C.

172 Scipio Africanus and the beautiful maiden: 210 B.C. Cf. Livy XXVI.50; Val. Max. IV.III.1; Gell. VII.8; Polyb. X.19.

173 Alexander and the beautiful maiden: Cf. Gell. VII.8; Ammian. Marc. XXIV.IV.27.

174 the Emperor Caesar Augustus Germanicus: Domitian.

175 Domitian orders compensation to be paid for the crops of the Cubii: 83 A.D.

176 Titus Quinctius' trumpets: 468 B.C. Cf. Livy II.64-65.

177 Sertorius' surprise for an overconfident cavalry: 80-72 B.C.

178 Chares' phantom reinforcements: 366-338 B.C.

179 Iphicrates' watch-fires: 389 B.C. This same story is told in I.V.24. Cf. also Polyaen. III.IX.41, 46, 50.

180 the Gauls scatter their gold: Cic. Pro Lege Manil. ix.22 and Flor. III.V.18 attribute a similar stratagem to Mithridates.

181 Tryphon scatters money: 134 B.C.

182 Sertorius' army melts away to re-form elsewhere: 75 B.C. Cf. Plut. Pomp. 19.

183 Viriathus' army melts away to re-form elsewhere: 147-139 B.C. Cf. Appian Hisp. 62. Cf. note to II.V.7.

184 Horatius Cocles holds the bridge: 507 B.C. Cf. Livy II.10; Dionys. V.23-25; Plut. Publ. 16.

185 Afranius takes a break, but it was a short one: 49 B.C. Cf. Caes. B.C. I.80.

186 Anthony sets up camp: 36 B.C.

187 Philip's truce to bury the dead: 198 B.C.

188 Publius Claudius celebrates victory: 249 B.C. Battle of Drepanum. Eutrop. II.26, Polyb. I.LI.11-12, and Oros. IV.X.3, give the number of ships as thirty.

Book III

If the preceding books have corresponded to their titles, and I have held the attention of the reader up to this point, I will now treat of ruses that deal with the siege and defence of towns. Waiving any preface, I will first submit those which are useful in the siege of cities, then those which offer suggestions to the besieged. Laying aside also all considerations of works and engines of war, the invention of which has long since reached its limit,1 and for the improvement of which I see no further hope in the applied arts, I shall recognize the following types of stratagems connected with siege operations:

I. On surprise attacks.
II. On deceiving the besieged.
III. On inducing treachery.
IV. By what means the enemy may be reduced to want.
V. How to persuade the enemy that the siege will be maintained.
VI. On distracting the attention of a hostile garrison.
VII. On diverting streams and contaminating waters.
VIII. On terrorizing the besieged.
IX. On attacks from an unexpected quarter.
X. On setting traps to draw out the besieged.
XI. On pretended retirements.

On the other hand, stratagems connected with the protection of the besieged:

XII. On stimulating the vigilance of one's own troops.
XIII. On sending and receiving messages.
XIV. On introducing reinforcements and supplying provisions.
XV. How to produce the impression of abundance of what is lacking.
XVI. How to meet the menace of treason and desertion.
XVII. On sorties.
XVIII. Concerning steadfastness on the part of the besieged.

I. On Surprise Attacks

1 The consul Titus Quinctius, having conquered the Aequians and Volscians in an engagement, decided to storm the walled town of Antium. Accordingly he called an assembly of the soldiers and explained how necessary this project was and how easy, if only it were not postponed. Then, having roused enthusiasm by his address, he assaulted the town.2

2 Marcus Cato, when in Spain, saw that he could gain possession of a certain town, if only he could assault the enemy by surprise. Accordingly, having in two days accomplished a four days' march through rough and barren districts, he crushed his foes, who were fearing no such event. Then, when his men asked the reason of so easy a success, he told them that they had won the victory as soon as they had accomplished the four days' march in two.3

II. On Deceiving the Besieged

1 When Domitius Calvinus was besieging Lueria, a town of the Ligurians, protected not only by its location and siege-works, but also by the superiority of its defenders, he instituted the practice of marching frequently round the walls with all his forces, and then marching back to camp. When the townspeople had been induced by this routine to believe that the Roman

commander did this for the purpose of drill, and consequently took no precautions against his efforts, he transformed this practice of parading into a sudden attack, and gaining possession of the walls, forced the inhabitants to surrender.

2 The consul Gaius Duellius, by frequently exercising his soldiers and sailors, succeeded in preventing the Carthaginians from taking notice of a practice which was innocent enough, until suddenly he brought up his fleet and seized their fortifications.4

3 Hannibal captured many cities in Italy by sending ahead certain of his own men, dressed in the garb of Romans and speaking Latin, which they had acquired as a result of long experience in the war.5

4 The Arcadians, when besieging a stronghold of the Messenians, fabricated certain weapons to resemble those of the enemy. Then, at the time when they learned that another force was to relieve the first, they dressed themselves in the uniform of those who were expected, and being admitted as comrades in consequence of this confusion, they secured possession of the place and wrought havoc among the foe.

5 Cimon, the Athenian general, having designs on a certain city in Caria, under cover of night set fire to a temple of Diana, held in high reverence by the inhabitants, and also to a grove outside the walls. Then, when the townspeople poured out to fight the conflagration, Cimon captured the city, since it was left without defenders.6

6 Alcibiades, the Athenian commander, while besieging the strongly fortified city of the Agrigentines, requested a conference of the citizens, and, as though discussing matters of common concern, addressed them at length in the theatre, where according to the custom of the Greeks it was usual to afford a place for consultation. Then, while he held the crowd on the pretence of deliberation, the Athenians, whom he had previously prepared for this move, captured the city, thus left unguarded.7

7 When Epaminondas, the Theban, was campaigning in Arcadia, and on a certain holiday the women of the enemy strolled in large numbers outside the walls, he sent among them a number of his own troops dressed in women's attire. In consequence of this disguise, the men were admitted towards nightfall to the town, whereupon they seized it and threw it open to their companions.8

8 Aristippus, the Spartan, on a holiday of the Tegeans, when the whole population had gone out of the city to celebrate the rites of Minerva, sent to Tegea a number of mules laden with grain-bags filled with chaff. The mules were driven by soldiers disguised as traders, who, escaping notice, threw open the gates of the town to their comrades.

9 When Antiochus was besieging the fortified town of Suenda in Cappadocia, he intercepted some beasts of burden which had gone out to procure grain. Then, killing their attendants, he dressed his own soldiers in their clothes and sent them in as though bringing p213back the grain. The sentinels fell into the trap and, mistaking the soldiers for teamsters, let the troops of Antiochus enter the fortifications.

10 When the Thebans were unable by the utmost exertions to gain possession of the harbour of the Sicyonians, they filled a large vessel with armed men, exhibiting a cargo in full view on deck, in order, under the guise of traders, to deceive their enemies. Then at a point of the fortifications remote from the sea they stationed a few men, with whom certain unarmed members of the crew upon disembarking were to engage in a fracas, on the pretence of a

quarrel. When the Sicyonians were summoned to stop the altercation, the Theban crews seized both the unguarded harbour and the town.9

11 Timarchus, the Aetolian, having killed Charmades, general of King Ptolemy,10 arrayed himself in Macedonian fashion in the cloak and casque of the slain commander. Through this disguise he was admitted as Charmades into the harbour of the Sanii and secured possession of it.

III. On Inducing Treachery

1 When the consul Papirius Cursor was before Tarentum, and Milo was holding the town with a force of Epirotes, Papirius promised safety to Milo and the townspeople if he should secure possession of the town through Milo's agency. Bribed by these inducements, Milo persuaded the Tarentines to send him as ambassador to the consul, from whom, in conformity with their understanding, he brought back liberal promises by means of which he caused the citizens to relapse into a feeling of security, and was thus enabled to hand the city over to Cursor, since it was left unguarded.11

2 Marcus Marcellus, having tempted a certain Sosistratus of Syracuse to turn traitor, learned from him that the guards would be less strict on a holiday when a certain citizen named Epicydes was to make a generous distribution of wine and food. So, taking advantage of the gaiety and the consequent laxness of discipline, he scaled the walls, slew the sentinels, and threw open to the Roman army a city already made famous as the scene of noted victories.12

3 When Tarquinius Superbus was unable to induce Gabii to surrender, he scourged his son Sextus with rods and sent him among the enemy, where he arraigned the cruelty of his father and persuaded the Gabians to utilize his hatred against the king. Accordingly he was chosen leader in the war, and delivered Gabii over to his father.13

4 Cyrus, king of the Persians, having proved the loyalty of his attendant Zopyrus, deliberately mutilated his face and sent him among the enemy. In consequence of their belief in his wrongs, he was regarded as implacably hostile to Cyrus, and promoted this belief by running up and discharging his weapons against Cyrus, whenever an engagement took place, till finally the city of the Babylonians was entrusted to him and by him delivered into the hands of Cyrus.14

5 Philip, when prevented from gaining possession of the town of the Sanians, bribed one of their generals, Apollonides, to turn traitor, inducing him to plant a cart laden with dressed stone at the very entrance to the gate. Then straightway giving the signal, he followed after the townspeople, who were huddled in panic around the blocked entrance of the gate, and succeeded in overwhelming them.15

6 When Hannibal was before Tarentum, and this town was held by a Roman garrison under the command of Livius, he induced a certain Cononeus of Tarentum to turn traitor, and concerted with him a stratagem whereby he was to go out at night for the purpose of hunting, on the ground that enemy rendered this impossible by day. When he went forth, Hannibal supplied him with boars to present to Livius as trophies of the chase. When this had repeatedly been done, and for that reason was less noticed, Hannibal one night dressed a number of Carthaginians in the garb of hunters and introduced them among Cononeus's attendants. When these men, loaded with the game they were carrying, were admitted by the guards, they straightway attacked and slew the latter. Then breaking down the gate, they admitted Hannibal with his troops, who slew all the Romans, save those who had fled for refuge to the citadel.16

7 When Lysimachus, king of the Macedonians, was besieging the Ephesians, these were assisted by the pirate chief Mandro, who was in the habit of bringing into Ephesus galleys laden with booty. Accordingly Lysimachus bribed Mandro to turn traitor, and attached to him a number of dauntless Macedonians to be taken into the city as captives, with hands pinioned behind their backs. These men subsequently snatched weapons from the citadel and delivered the town into the hands of Lysimachus.17

IV. By What Means the Enemy may be Reduced to Want.

1 Fabius Maximus, having laid waste the lands of the Campanians, in order that they might have nothing left to warrant the confidence that a siege could be sustained, withdrew at the time of the sowing, that inhabitants might plant what seed they had remaining. Then, returning, he destroyed the new crop and thus made himself master of the Campanians, whom he had reduced to famine.18

2 Antigonus employed the same device against the Athenians.19

3 Dionysius, having captured many cities and wishing to attack the Rhegians, who were well provided with supplies, pretended to desire peace, and begged of them to furnish provisions for his army. When he had secured his request and had consumed the grain of the inhabitants, he attacked their town, now stripped of food, and conquered it.20

4 He is said to have employed the same device also against the people of Himera.21

5 When Alexander22 was about to besiege Leucadia, a town well-supplied with provisions, he first captured the fortresses on the border and allowed all the people from these to flee for refuge to Leucadia, in order that the food-supplies might be consumed with greater rapidity when shared by many.

6 Phalaris of Agrigentum, when besieging certain places in Sicily protected by fortifications, pretended to make a treaty and deposited with the Sicilians all the wheat which he said he had remaining, taking pains, however, that the chambers of the buildings in which the grain was stored should have leaky roofs. Then when the Sicilians, relying on the wheat which Phalaris had deposited with them, had used up their own supplies, Phalaris attacked them at the beginning of summer and as a result of their lack of provisions forced them to surrender.23

V. How to Persuade the Enemy that the Siege will be Maintained

1 When Clearchus, the Spartan, had learned that the Thracians had conveyed to the mountains all things necessary for their subsistence and were buoyed up by the sole hope that he would withdraw in consequence of lack of supplies, at the time when he surmised their envoys would come, he ordered one of the prisoners to be put to death in full view and his body to be distributed in pieces among the tents, as though for the mess. The Thracians, believing that Clearchus would stick at nothing in order to hold out, since he brought himself to try such loathsome food, delivered themselves up.24

2 When the Lusitanians told Tiberius Gracchus that they had supplies for ten years and for that reason stood in no fear of a siege, he answered: "Then I'll capture you in the eleventh year." Terror-stricken by this language, the Lusitanians, though well supplied with provisions, at once surrendered.25

3 When Aulus Torquatus was besieging a Greek city and was told that the young men of the city were engaged in earnest practice with the javelin and bow, he replied: "Then the price at which I shall presently sell them shall be higher."

VI. On Distracting the Attention of a Hostile Garrison

1 When Hannibal had returned to Africa, many towns were still held by strong forces of the Carthaginians. Scipio's policy demanded that these towns should be reduced. Accordingly he often sent troops to assault them. Finally he would appear before the towns as though bent on sacking them, and would then retire, feigning fear. Hannibal, thinking his alarm real, withdrew the garrison from all points, and began to follow, as though determined to fight a decisive battle. Scipio, having thus accomplished what he intended, with the assistance of Masinissa and the Numidians, captured the towns, which had thus been stripped of their defenders.26

2 Publius Cornelius Scipio, appreciating the difficulty of capturing Delminus, because it was defended by the concerted efforts of the population of the district, began to assault other towns. Then, when the inhabitants of the various towns had been called back to defend their homes, Scipio took Delminus, which had been left without support.27

3 Pyrrhus, king of Epirus, in his war against the Illyrians, aimed to reduce their capital, but despairing of this, began to attack the other towns, and succeeded in making the enemy disperse to protect their other cities, since they had confidence in the apparently adequate fortification of the capital. When he had accomplished this, he recalled his own forces and captured the town, now left without defenders.28

4 The consul Cornelius Rufinus for some time besieged the city of Crotona, without success, since it had been made impregnable by the arrival of a band of Lucanian reinforcements. He therefore pretended to desist from his undertaking, and by offers of great rewards induced a certain prisoner to go to Crotona. This emissary, by feigning to have escaped from custody, persuaded the inhabitants to believe his report that the Romans had withdrawn. The people of Crotona, thinking this to be true, dismissed their allies. Then, weakened by being stripped of their defenders, they were surprised and captured.29

5 Mago, general of the Carthaginians, having defeated Gnaeus Piso and having blockaded the tower wherein he had taken refuge, suspecting that reinforcements would come to his relief, sent a deserter to persuade the approaching troops that Piso was already captured. Having thus scared them off, Mago made his victory complete.30

6 Alcibiades, wishing to capture the city of Syracuse in Sicily, chose from among the people of Catana, where he was encamped, a certain man of tested shrewdness and sent him to the Syracusans. This man, when brought before the public assembly of the Syracusans, persuaded them that the people of Catana were very hostile to the Athenians, and that, if assisted by the Syracusans, they would crush the Athenians and Alcibiades along with them. Induced by these representations, the Syracusans left their own city and set out in full force to join the people of Catana, whereupon Alcibiades attacked Syracuse from the rear, and finding it unprotected, as he had hoped, brought it under subjection.31

7 When the people of Troezen were held in subjection by troops under the command of Craterus, the Athenian Cleonymus made an assault on the town and hurled within its walls missiles inscribed with messages stating that Cleonymus had come to liberate their state. At the same time certain prisoners whom he had won over to his side were sent back to disparage

Craterus. By this plan he stirred up internal strife among the besieged and, bringing up his troops, gained possession of the city.32

VII. On Diverting Streams and Contaminating Waters

1 Publius Servilius diverted the stream from which the inhabitants of Isaura drew their water, and thus forced them to surrender in consequence of thirst.33

2 Gaius Caesar, in one of his Gallic campaigns, deprived the city of the Cadurcia of water, although it was surrounded by a river and abounded in springs; for he diverted the springs by subterranean channels, while his archers shut off all access to the river.34

3 Lucius Metellus, when fighting in Hither Spain, diverted the course of a river and directed it from a higher level against the camp of the enemy, which was located on low ground. Then, when the enemy were in a panic from the sudden flood, he had them slain by men whom he had stationed in ambush for this very purpose.35

4 At Babylon, which is divided into two parts by the river Euphrates, Alexander constructed both a ditch and an embankment, the enemy supposing that the earth was being taken out merely to form the embankment. Alexander, accordingly, suddenly diverting the stream, entered the town along the former river bed, which had dried up and thus afforded an entrance to the town.36

5 Semiramis is said to have done the same thing in the war against the Babylonians, by diverting the same Euphrates.

6 Clisthenes of Sicyon cut the water-pipes leading into the town of the Crisaeans. Then when the townspeople were suffering from thirst, he turned on the water again, now poisoned with hellebore. When the inhabitants used this, they were so weakened by diarrhoea that Clisthenes overcame them.37

VIII. On Terrorizing the Besieged

1 When Philip was unable by the utmost exertions to capture the fortress of Prinassus, he made excavations of earth directly in front of the walls and pretended to be constructing a tunnel. The men within the fortress, imagining that they were being undermined, surrendered.38

2 Pelopidas, the Theban, on one occasion planned to make a simultaneous attack on two towns of the Magnetes, not very far distant from each other. As he advanced against one of these towns, he gave orders that, in accordance with preconcerted arrangements, four horsemen should come from the other camp with garlands on their heads and with the marked eagerness of those who announce a victory. To complete the illusion, he arranged to have a forest between the two cities set on fire, to give the appearance of a burning town. Besides this, he ordered certain prisoners to be led along, dressed in the costume of the townspeople. When the besieged had been terrified by these demonstrations, deeming themselves already defeated in one quarter, they ceased to offer resistance.39

3 Cyrus, king of the Persians, at one time forced Croesus to take refuge in Sardis. On one side a steep hill prevented access to the town. Here near the walls Cyrus erected masts equal to the height of the ridge of the hill, and on them placed dummies of armed men dressed in Persian uniforms. At night he brought these to the hill. Then at dawn he attacked the walls from the other side. As soon as the sun rose and the dummies, flashing in the sunlight, revealed the garb

of warriors, the townspeople, imagining that their city had been captured from the rear, scattered in flight and left the field to the enemy.40

IX. On Attacks from an Unexpected Quarter

1 Scipio, when fighting before Carthage, approached the walls of the city, just before the turn of the tide, guided, as he said, by some god. Then, when the tide went out in the shallow lagoon, he burst in at that point, the enemy not expecting him there.41

2 Fabius Maximus, son of Fabius Cunctator, finding Arpi occupied by Hannibal's forces, first inspected the site of the town, and then sent six hundred soldiers on a dark night to mount the walls with scaling-ladders at a part of the town which was fortified and therefore less guarded, and to tear down the gates. These men were aided in the execution of their orders by the noise of the falling rain, which deadened the sound of their operations. In another quarter, Fabius himself made an attack at a given signal and captured Arpi.42

3 In the Jugurthine War Gaius Marius was at one time besieging a fortress situated near the Mulucha river. It stood on a rocky eminence, accessible on one side by a single narrow path, while the other side, as though by special design, was precipitous. It happened that a certain Ligurian, a common soldier from among the auxiliaries, had gone out to procure water, and, while gathering snails among the rocks of the mountain, had reached the summit. This man reported to Marius that it was possible to clamber up to the stronghold. Marius accordingly sent a few centurions in company with his fleetest soldiers, including also the most skilful trumpeters. These men went bare-headed and bare-footed, that they might see better and make their way more easily over the rocks; their shields and swords were fastened to their backs. Guided by the Ligurian, and aided by straps and staffs, with which they support themselves, they made their way up to the rear of the fortress, which, owing to its position, was without defenders, and then began to sound their trumpets and make a great uproar, as they had previously been directed. At this signal, Marius, steadfastly urging on his men, began to advance with renewed fury against the defenders of the fortress. The latter were recalled from the defence by the populace, who had lost heart under the impression that the town had been captured from the rear, so that Marius was enabled to press on and capture the fort.43

4 The consul Lucius Cornelius Rufinus captured numerous towns in Sardinia by landing powerful detachments of troops at night, with instructions to remain in hiding and to wait till he himself drew near to land with his ships. Then as the enemy came to meet him at his approach, he led them a long chase by pretending to flee, while his other troops attacked the cities thus abandoned by their inhabitants.44

5 Pericles, the Athenian general, was once besieging a city which was protected by very determined defenders. At night he ordered the trumpet to be sounded and a loud outcry to be raised at a quarter of the walls adjacent to the sea. The enemy, thinking that the town had been entered at that point, abandoned the gates, whereupon, as soon as these were left without defence, Pericles burst into the town.

6 Alcibiades, the Athenian general, planning to assault Cyzicus, approached the town unexpectedly at night, and commanded his trumpeters to sound their instruments at a different part of the fortifications. The defenders of the walls were ample, but since they all flocked to the side where alone they imagined themselves to be attacked, Alcibiades succeeded in scaling the walls at the point where there was no resistance.45

7 Thrasybulus, general of the Milesians, in his efforts to seize the harbour of the Sicyonians, made repeated attacks upon the inhabitants from the land side. Then, when the enemy directed their attention to the point where they were attacked, he suddenly seized the harbour with his fleet.46

8 Philip, while besieging a certain coast town, secretly lashed ships together in pairs, with a common deck over all, and erected towers on them. Then launching an attack with other towers by land, he distracted the attention of the defenders of the city, till he brought up by sea the ships provided with towers, and advanced against the walls at the point where no resistance was offered.

9 Pericles, when about to lay siege to a fortress of the Peloponnesians to which there were only two avenues of approach, cut off one of these by a trench and began to fortify the other. The defenders of the fortress, thrown off their guard at one point, began to watch only the other where they saw the building going on. But Pericles, having prepared bridges, laid them across the trench and entered the fortress at the point where no guard was kept.47

10 Antiochus, when fighting against the Ephesians, directed the Rhodians, whom he had as allies, to make an attack on the harbour at night with a great uproar. When the entire population rushed headlong to this quarter, leaving the rest of the fortress without defenders, Antiochus attacked at a different quarter and captured the town.

X. On Setting Traps to Draw out the Besieged

1 When Cato was besieging the Lacetani, he sent away in full view of the enemy all his other troops, while ordering certain Suessetani, who were the least martial of his allies, to attack the walls of the town. When the Lacetani, making a sortie, easily repulsed these forces and pursued them eagerly as they fled, the soldiers whom Cato had placed in hiding rose up and by their help he captured the town.48

2 When campaigning in Sardinia, Lucius Scipio, in order to draw out the defenders of a certain city, abandoned the siege which he had begun, and pretended to flee with a detachment of his troops. Then, when the inhabitants followed him pell-mell, he attacked the town with the help of those whom he had placed in hiding near at hand.49

3 When Hannibal was besieging the city of Himera, he purposely allowed his camp to be captured, ordering the Carthaginians to retire, on the ground that the enemy were superior. The inhabitants were so deceived by this turn of affairs that in their joy they came out of the city and advanced against the Carthaginian breast-works, whereupon Hannibal, finding the town vacant, captured it by means of the troops whom he had placed in ambush for this very contingency.50

4 In order to draw out the Saguntines, Hannibal on a certain occasion advanced against their walls with a thin line of troops. Then, at the first sally of the inhabitants, feigning flight, he withdrew, and interposing troops between the pursuing foe and the city, he slaughtered the enemy thus cut off from their fellows between the two forces.51

5 Himilco, the Carthaginian, when campaigning near Agrigentum, placed part of his forces in ambush near the town, and directed them to set fire to some damp wood as soon as the soldiers from the town should come forth. Then, advancing at daybreak with the rest of his army for the purpose of luring forth the enemy, he feigned flight and drew the inhabitants after him for a considerable distance by his retirement. The men in ambush near the walls applied the torch

to the wood-piles as directed. The Agrigentines, beholding the smoke ascend, thought their city on fire and ran back in alarm to protect it. Being encountered by those lying in wait for them near the walls, and beset in the rear by those whom they had just been pursuing, they were caught between two forces and so cut to pieces.52

6 Viriathus, on one occasion, having placed men in ambush, sent a few others to drive off the flocks of the Segobrigenses. When the latter rushed out in great numbers to defend their flocks and followed up the marauders, who pretended to flee, they were drawn into an ambush and cut to pieces.53

7 When Lucullus was put in charge of a garrison of two cohorts at Heraclea, the cavalry of the Scordisci, by pretending to drive off the flocks of the inhabitants, provoked a sortie. Then, when Lucullus followed, they drew him into an ambush, feigning flight, and killed him together with eight hundred of his followers.

8 The Athenian general, Chares, when about to attack a city on the coast, hid his fleet behind certain promontories and then ordered his swiftest ship to sail past the forces of the enemy. At sight of this ship, all the forces guarding the harbour darted out in pursuit, whereat Chares sailed in with the rest of his fleet and took possession of the undefended harbour and likewise of the city itself.54

9 On one occasion when Roman troops were blockading Lilybaeum by land and sea, Barca, general of the Carthaginians in Sicily, ordered a part of his fleet to appear in the offing ready for action. When our men darted out at the sight of this, Barca seized the harbour of Lilybaeum with the ships which he had held in hiding.55

XI. On Pretended Retirements

1 When the Athenian general Phormio had ravaged the lands of the Chalcidians, and their envoys complained of this action, he answered them graciously, and at evening, when he was about to dismiss them, pretended that a letter had come from his fellow-citizens requiring his return. Accordingly he retired a short distance and dismissed the envoys. When these reported that all was safe and that Phormio had withdrawn, the Chalcidians in view of the promised consideration and of the withdrawal of the troops, relaxed the guard of their town. Than Phormio suddenly returned and the Chalcidians were unable to withstand his unexpected attack.56

2 When the Spartan commander, Agesilaus, was blockading the Phocaeans and had learned that those who were then lending them support were weary with the burdens of war, he retired a short distance as though for other objects, thus leaving the allies free opportunity to withdraw. Not long after, bringing back his troops, he defeated the Phocaeans thus left without assistance.57

3 When fighting against the Byzantines, who kept within their walls, Alcibiades laid an ambush and, feigning a retirement, took them off their guard and crushed them.58

4 Viriathus, after retreating for three days, suddenly turned round and traversed the same distance in one day. He thus crushed the Segobrigenses, taking them off their guard at a moment when they were earnestly engaged in sacrifice.59

5 In the operations around Mantinea, Epaminondas, having noticed that the Spartans had come to help his enemies, conceived the idea that Sparta might be captured, if he should set out

against it secretly. Accordingly he ordered numerous watch-fires to be built at night, that, by appearing to remain, he might conceal his departure. But betrayed by a deserter and pursued by the Lacedaemonian troops, he abandoned his march to Sparta, and employed the same scheme against the Mantineans; for by building watch-fires as before, he deceived the Spartans into thinking that he would remain. Meanwhile, returning to Mantinea by a march of forty miles, he found it without defences and captured it.60

On the other hand, Stratagems Connected with the Protection of the Besieged

XII. On Stimulating the Vigilance of One's Own Troops

1 Alcibiades, the Athenian commander, when his own city was blockaded by the Spartans, fearing negligence on the part of the guards, ordered the men on picket-duty to watch for the light which he should exhibit from the citadel at night, and to raise their own lights at sight of it, threatening that whoever failed in this duty should suffer a penalty. While anxiously awaiting the signal of their general, all maintained constant watch, and so escaped the dangers of the perilous night.61

2 When Iphicrates, the Athenian general, was holding Corinth with a garrison and on one occasion personally made the rounds of the sentries as the enemy were approaching, he found one of the guards asleep at his post and stabbed him with his spear. When certain ones rebuked this procedure as cruel, he answered: "I left him as I found him."62

3 Epaminondas the Theban is said, on one occasion, to have done the same thing.

XIII. On Sending and Receiving Messages

1 When the Romans were besieged in the Capitol, they sent Pontius Cominius to implore Camillus to come to their aid. Pontius, to elude the pickets of the Gauls, let himself down over the Tarpeian Rock, swam the Tiber, and reached Veii. Having accomplished his errand, he returned by the same route to his friends.63

2 When the Romans were maintaining careful guard against the inhabitants of Capua, whom they were besieging, the latter sent a certain fellow in the guise of a deserter, and he, finding an opportunity to escape, conveyed to the Carthaginians a letter which he had secreted in his belt.64

3 Some have written messages on skins and then sewed these to the carcasses of game or sheep.

4 Some have stuffed the message under the tail of a mule while passing the picket-posts.

5 Some have written on the linings of scabbards.

6 When the Cyzicenes were besieged by Mithridates, Lucius Lucullus wished to inform them of his approach. There was a single narrow entrance to the city, connecting the island with the mainland by a small bridge. Since this was held by forces of the enemy, he sewed some letters up inside two inflated skins and then ordered one of his soldiers, an adept in swimming and boating, to mount the skins, which he had fastened together at the bottom by two strips some distance apart, and to make the trip of •seven miles across. So skilfully did the soldier do this that, by spreading his legs, he steered his course as though by rudder, and deceived those watching from a distance by appearing to be some marine creature.65

7 The consul Hirtius often sent letters inscribed on lead plates to Decimus Brutus, who was besieged by Antonius at Mutina. The letters were fastened to the arms of soldiers, who then swam across the Scultenna River.66

8 Hirtius also shut up pigeons in the dark, starved them, fastened letters to their necks by a hair, and then released them as near to the city walls as he could. The birds, eager for light and food, sought the highest buildings and were received by Brutus, who in that way was informed of everything, especially after he set food in certain spots and taught the pigeons to alight there.67

XIV. On Introducing Reinforcements and Supplying Provisions

1 In the Civil War, when the Spanish city of Ategua, belonging to Pompey's party, was under blockade, one night a Moor, pretending to be a tribune's adjutant belonging to the Caesarian party, roused certain sentries and got from them the password. He then roused others, and by continuing his deception, succeeded in conducting reinforcements for Pompey through the midst of Caesar's troops.68

2 When Hannibal was besieging Casilinum, the Romans sent big jars of wheat down the current of the Volturnus, to be picked up by the besieged. After Hannibal stopped these by throwing a chain across the river, the Romans scattered nuts on the water. These floated down stream to the city and thus sustained the necessities of the allies.69

3 When the inhabitants of Mutina were blockaded by Antonius, and were greatly in need of salt, Hirtius packed some in jars and sent it in to them by way of the Scultenna River.70

4 Hirtius also sent down the river carcasses of sheep, which were received and thus furnished the necessities of life.

XV. How to Produce the Impression of Abundance of what is Lacking

1 When the Capitol was besieged by the Gauls, the Romans, in the extremity of famine, threw bread among the enemy. They thus produced the impression that they were well supplied with food, and so withstood the siege till Camillus came.71

2 The Athenians are said to have employed the same ruse against the Spartans.

3 The inhabitants of Casilinum, when blockaded by Hannibal, were thought to have reached the starvation point, since Hannibal had cut off from their food supply even their use of the growing herbs by ploughing the ground between his camp and the city walls. The ground being thus made ready, the besieged° flung seed into it, thus giving the impression that they had enough wherewith to sustain life even till harvest time.72

4 When the survivors of the Varian disaster73 were under siege and seemed to be running short of food, they spent an entire night in leading prisoners round their store-houses; then, having cut off their hands, they turned them loose. These men persuaded the besieging force to cherish no hope of an early reduction of the Romans by starvation, since they had an abundance of food supplies.

5 When the Thracians were besieged on a steep mountain inaccessible to the enemy, they got together by individual contributions a small amount of wheat. This they fed to a few sheep which they then drove among the forces of the enemy. When the sheep had been caught and slaughtered, and traces of wheat had been found in their intestines, the enemy raised the siege, imagining that the Thracians had a surplus of wheat, inasmuch as they fed it even to their sheep.

7 The Milesians were at one time suffering a long siege at the hands of Alyattes, who hoped they could be starved into surrender. But the Milesian commander, Thrasybulus, in anticipation of the arrival of envoys from Alyattes, ordered all the grain to be brought together into the market-place, arranged for banquets to be held on that occasion, and provided sumptuous feasts throughout the city. Thus he convinced the enemy that the Milesians had abundance of provisions with which to sustain a long siege.74

XVI. How to Meet the Menace of Treason and Desertion

1 A certain Lucius Bantius of Nola on one occasion cherished the plan of rousing his fellow-citizens to revolt, as a favour to Hannibal, by whose kindness he had been tended when wounded among those engaged at Cannae, and by whom he had been sent back from captivity to his own people. Claudius Marcellus, learning of his purpose and not daring to put him to death, for fear that by his punishment he would stir up the rest of the people of Nola, summoned Bantius and talked with him, pronouncing him a very valiant soldier (a fact which Marcellus admitted he had not previously known), and urging him to remain with him. Besides these compliments, he presented him also with a horse. By such kindness he secured the loyalty, not only of Bantius, but also of his townspeople, since their allegiance hinged on his.75

2 When the Gallic auxiliaries of Hamilcar, the Carthaginian general, were in the habit of crossing over to the Romans and were regularly received by them as allies, Hamilcar engaged his most loyal men to pretend desertion, while actually they slew the Romans who came out to welcome them. This device was not merely of present aid to Hamilcar, but caused real deserters to be regarded in future as objects of suspicion in the eyes of the Romans.76

3 Hanno, commander of the Carthaginians in Sicily, learned on one occasion that about four thousand Gallic mercenaries had conspired to desert to the Romans, because for several months they had received no pay. Not daring to punish them, for fear of mutiny, he promised to make good the deferred payment by increasing their wages. When the Gauls rendered thanks for this, Hanno, promising that they should be permitted to go out foraging at a suitable time, sent to the consul Otacilius an extremely trustworthy steward, who pretended to have deserted on account of embezzlement, and who reported that on the coming night four thousand Gauls, sent out on a foraging expedition, could be captured. Otacilius, not immediately crediting the deserter, nor yet thinking the matter ought to be treated with disdain, placed the pick of his men in ambush. These met the Gauls, who fulfilled Hanno's purpose in a twofold manner, since they not only slew a number of the Romans, but were themselves slaughtered to the last man.77

4 By a similar plan Hannibal took vengeance on certain deserters; for, being aware that some of his soldiers had deserted on the previous night, and knowing that spies of the enemy were in his camp, he publicly proclaimed that the name of "deserter" ought not to be applied to his cleverest soldiers, who at his order had gone out to learn the designs of the enemy. The spies,

as soon as they heard this pronouncement, reported it to their own side. Thereupon the deserters were arrested by the Romans and sent back with their hands cut off.

5 When Diodotus was holding Amphipolis with a garrison, and entertained suspicions of two thousand Thracians, who seemed likely to pillage the city, he invented the story that a few hostile ships had put in at the shore nearby and could be plundered. When he had incited the Thracians at that prospect, he let them out. Then, closing the gates, he refused to admit them again.78

XVII. On Sorties

1 When Hasdrubal came to besiege Panormus, the Romans, who were in possession of the town, purposely placed a scanty number of defenders on the walls. In contempt of their small numbers, Hasdrubal incautiously approached the walls, whereupon they made a sortie and slew him.79

2 When the Ligurians with their entire force made a surprise attack on the camp of Aemilius Paulus, the latter feigned fear and for a long time kept his troops in camp. Then, when the enemy were exhausted, making a sortie by the four gates, he defeated the Ligurians and made them prisoners.80

3 Livius, commander of the Romans, when holding the citadel of the Tarentines, sent envoys to Hasdrubal, requesting the privilege of withdrawing undisturbed. When by this feint he had thrown the enemy off their guard, he made a sortie and cut them to pieces.81

4 Gnaeus Pompey, when besieged near Dyrrhachium, not only released his own men from blockade, but also made a sally at an opportune time and place; for just as Caesar was making a fierce assault on a fortified position surrounded by a double line of works, Pompey, by this sortie, so enveloped him with a cordon of troops that Caesar incurred no slight peril and loss, caught, as he was, between those whom he was besieging and those who had surrounded him from the outside.82

5 Flavius Fimbria, when fighting in Asia near the river Rhyndacus against the son of Mithridates, constructed two lines of works on his flanks and a ditch in front, and kept his soldiers quietly within their entrenchments, until the cavalry of the enemy passed within the confined portions of his fortifications. Then, making a sortie, he slew six thousand of them.83

6 When the forces of Titurius Sabinus and Cotta, Caesar's lieutenants in Gaul, had been wiped out by Ambiorix, Caesar was urged by Quintus Cicero, who was himself also under siege, to come with two legions to his relief. The enemy then turned upon Caesar, who feigned fear and kept his troops within his camp, which he had purposely constructed on a smaller scale than usual. The Gauls, already counting on victory, and pressing forward as though to plunder the camp, began to fill up the ditches and to tear down the ramparts. Caesar, therefore, as the Gauls were not equipped for battle, suddenly sent forth his own troops from all quarters and cut the enemy to pieces.84

7 When Titurius Sabinus was fighting against a large force of Gauls, he kept his troops within their fortifications, and thus produced upon the Gauls the impression that he was afraid. To further this impression, he sent a deserter to state that the Roman army was in despair and was planning to flee. Spurred on by the hope of victory thus offered, the Gauls loaded themselves with wood and brush with which to fill the trenches, and at top speed started for our camp,

which was pitched on the top of an elevation. From there Titurius launched all his forces against them, killing many of the Gauls and receiving large numbers in surrender.85

8 As Pompey was about to assault the town of Asculum the inhabitants exhibited on the ramparts a few aged and feeble men. Having thus thrown the Romans off their guard, they made a sortie and put them to flight.86

9 When the Numantines were blockaded, they did not even draw up a line of battle in front of the entrenchments, but kept so closely within the town that Popilius Laenas was emboldened to attack it with scaling-ladders. But, suspecting a ruse, since not even then was resistance offered, he recalled his men; whereupon the Numantines made a sortie and attacked the Romans in the rear as they were climbing down.87

XVIII. Concerning Steadfastness on the Part of the Besieged

1 The Romans, when Hannibal was encamped near their walls, in order to exhibit their confidence, sent troops out by a different gate to reinforce the armies which they had in Spain.88

2 The land on which Hannibal had his camp having come into the market owing to the death of the owner, the Romans bid the price up to the figure at which the property had sold before the war.88

3 When the Romans were besieged by Hannibal and were themselves besieging Capua, they passed a decree not to recall their army from the latter place until it was captured.89

The Editor's Notes:

1 the invention of works and engines of war has long since reached its limit: A curious illustration of the rashness of prophecy.

2 Titus Quinctius' rational pep talk: 468 B.C.

3 Cato's forced march: 195 B.C.

4 Duilius' naval exercises: 260 B.C.

5 Hannibal's infiltrators: 216-203 B.C.

6 Cimon sets fire to a temple of Diana: About 470 B.C.

7 Alcibiades' diversionary town meeting: 415 B.C. Thuc. VI.51, Polyaen. I.XL.4 and Diodor. XIII.IV.4, make Catana, and not Agrigentum, the scene of this stratagem.

8 Epaminondas' transvestites: 379 B.C. Polyaen. II.III.1 has a different version of this story, but in II.IV.3 attributes a somewhat similar stratagem to Pelopidas.

9 Thebans disguised as traders: Polyaen. V.XVI.3 makes Pammenes the author of this stratagem, 369 B.C.

10 King Ptolemy: Ptolemy Ceraunus, king of Macedonia, 280 B.C.

11 Papirius Cursor's quiet diplomacy: 272 B.C. Cf. **Zonar.** VIII.6.

12 Marcellus takes advantage of a holiday: 212 B.C. Livy XXV.23 ff., Plut. Marc. 18, and Polyaen. VIII.11 name Damippus a Spartan, rather than Sosistratus, as the source of the information.

13 Tarquinius Superbus scourges his son: Cf. Livy I.53; Val. Max. VII.IV.2; Polyaen. VIII.6.

14 Cyrus' mutilated aide: 518 B.C. Herod. III.153, **Justin.** I.X.15, and Polyaen. VII.13, represent Zopyrus as mutilating himself, and make **Darius** rather than Cyrus the monarch at the time.

15 Philip blocks a gate: 359-336 B.C.

16 Hannibal's generous hunters: 212 B.C. Cf. Appian Hann. 32; Livy XXV.8-9; Polyb. VIII.26. The name of the traitor is variously given.

17 Lysimachus infiltrates Ephesus: 287 B.C. Cf. **Polyaen.** V.19.

18 Fabius Maximus lets the enemy sow their crops: Apparently a confusion of two occasions. Cf. Livy XXIII.XLVIII.1-2 and XXV.XIII. 215 or 211 B.C.

19 Antigonus lets the enemy sow their crops: 263 B.C. Cf. Polyaen. IV.VI.20.

20 Dionysius gets supplies from Rhegium: 391 B.C. The version of Diodor. XIV.108 is slightly different.

21 Dionysius gets supplies from Himera: 387 B.C. Cf. **Polyaen.** V.II.10.

22 Alexander: Son of Pyrrhus. 266-263 B.C.

23 Phalaris' spoiled grain: 570-554 B.C. Cf. Polyaen. V.I.3. According to Polyaenus, the Sicilians were to return to Phalaris not the grain he had left with them but the crops from their later harvests.

24 Clearchus distributes rations to his cannibals: 402-401 B.C. Cf. Polyaen. II.II.8.

25 Tiberius Gracchus can wait: 179-178 B.C.

26 Scipio is clearly afraid to attack: 202 B.C.

27 Scipio goes after the enemy's allies: 155 B.C.

28 Pyrrhus goes after the enemy's allies: 296-280 B.C.

29 Cornelius Rufinus' disinformation: 277 B.C. Cf. **Zonar.** VIII.6.

30 Mago's disinformation: 216-203 B.C.

31 Alcibiades' shrewd talker: 415 B.C. This account agrees with that of Polyaen. I.XL.5. Thuc. VI.64 ff., and Diodor. XIII.VI.2 ff., attribute the stratagem to Nicias and Lamachus, and give a different version of its result.

32 Cleonymus' propaganda assault: 277-276 B.C. Polyaen. II.XXIX.1 calls Cleonymus a king of Sparta.

33 Publius Servilius diverts the enemy's water supply: 78-76 B.C.

34 Caesar diverts the enemy's water supply: 51 B.C. Cf. Hirt. B. G. VIII.40 ff.

35 Metellus floods the enemy's camp: 143-142 B.C. Quintus Caecilius Metellus Macedonicus, although the better manuscript readings give L. as the praenomen.

36 Alexander diverts a river: Herod. I.191, Xen. Cyrop. vii.5, and Polyaen. VII.VI.5, attribute this stratagem to Cyrus rather than Alexander.

37 Clisthenes poisons the enemy's water: 595-585 B.C. Polyaen. VI.13 attributes this stratagem to Eurylochus; Pausan. X.XXXVII.7, to Solon.

38 Philip's phantom mining: 201 B.C. Cf. Polyb. XVI.11; Polyaen. IV.XVIII.1.

39 Pelopidas' early victory: 369-364 B.C. Cf. Polyaen. II.IV.1.

40 Cyrus' dummies: 546 B.C. Cf. Polyaen. VII.VI.10; Ctes. ed. Müller, pp46-60. Herod. I.84 makes no mention of this stratagem.

41 Scipio uses the tides: 210 B.C. Cf. Livy XXVI.45-46; Polyb. X.10 ff.; Appian Hisp. 21 ff.

42 Fabius Maximus takes advantage of rain: 213 B.C. Cf. Livy XXIV.46-47.

43 Marius' mountain detachment: 107 B.C. Cf. Sall. Jug. 92-94; Flor. III.I.14.

44 Lucius Cornelius Rufinus's long chase: Probably a confusion of names: Lucius Cornelius Scipio invaded Sardinia in 259 B.C. (cf. III.X.2). Publius Cornelius Rufinus was consul in 277, but waged war only in Italy.

45 Alcibiades' diversionary trumpets: According to Thuc. VIII.107 and Diodor. XIII.XL.6, Cyzicus was not fortified by walls. This stratagem belongs rather to the taking of Byzantium, 409 B.C. Cf. III.XI.3; Diodor. XIII.66-67; Plut. Alcib. 31.

46 Thrasybulus' diversions: About 600 B.C.

47 Pericles' diversion: 430 B.C. Cf. I.V.10 and note.

48 Cato's diversion: 195 B.C. Cf. Livy XXXIV.20.

49 Lucius Scipio's diversion: 259 B.C. Cf. III.IX.4 and note.

50 Hannibal sacrifices his camp: 409 B.C. The Hannibal here mentioned is the son of Gisgo. Diodor. XIII.59-62 represents the Carthaginians as withdrawing in flight rather than executing a stratagem.

51 Hannibal's diversion at Sagunto: 219 B.C. Son of Hamilcar Barca. The identity of names led to the confusion between these two generals.

52 Himilco's diversion and ambush: 406 B.C. Cf. Polyaen. V.X.4. In the Old Testament (Josh. viii.), a similar stratagem is employed by Joshua.

53 Viriathus' diversion and ambush: 147-139 B.C.

54 Chares' diversion: 366-336 B.C.

55 Hamilcar Barca's diversion: 249 B.C. Cf. Polyb. I.44, where Hannibal, rather than Barca, is the general.

56 Phormio's feint: 432 B.C. Cf. Polyaen. III.IV.1.

57 Agesilaus' feint: 396-394 B.C. Cf. Polyaen. II.I.16.

58 Alcibiades draws out the enemy to ambush them: 409 B.C. Cf. Diodor. XIII.66-67; Plut. Alcib. 31.

59 Viriathus' speedy return: 147-139 B.C.

60 Epaminondas' phantom camps: 362 B.C. Cf. Polyb. IX.8; Diodor. XV.82-84; Plut. Ages. 34.

61 Alcibiades enforces watchfulness: Cf. Polyaen. I.XL.3.

62 "I left him as I found him": 393-391 B.C. Cf. Nep. Iphic. ii.1-2.

63 Pontius Cominius' triathlon: 390 B.C. Cf. Livy V.46; Diodor. XIV.116; Plut. Camill. 25.

64 the Capuans send a courier: 211 B.C. Livy XXVI.7 represents Hannibal as sending the letter to the Capuans.

65 Lucius Lucullus' special forces messenger: 74 B.C. Cf. Flor. III.V.15-16; Oros. VI.II.14.

66 Hirtius' special forces messengers: 43 B.C. Cf. Dio XLVI.36.

67 Hirtius' carrier pigeons: 43 B.C. Cf. Plin. N. H. X.37.

68 An African soldier of Pompey's gets the enemy password: 45 B.C. Cf. Dio XLIII.33-34. According to Dio, this man, Munatius Flaccus, whose real mission is to aid the Ateguans in withstanding the blockade of Caesar's troops, represents to the sentries that he has been sent by Caesar to betray the city. Thus having once learned the password, he secures an easy entrance into the city.

69 the Romans float food supplies to the besieged city of Casilinum: 216 B.C. Cf. Livy XXIII.19.

70 Hirtius floats food supplies to the besieged city of Mutina: 43 B.C.

71 the Romans throw bread among the enemy: 390 B.C. Cf. Livy V.48; Val. Max. VII.IV.3; Ovid. Fast. VI.350 ff.

72 the inhabitants of Casilinum sow seed: 216 B.C. Cf. Livy XXIII.19.

73 the Varian disaster: i.e. the defeat of Varus by Arminius in the Teutoburg Forest in 9 A.D.

74 Thrasybulus' feasts: About 611 B.C. Cf. Herod. I.21-22; Polyaen. VI.47.

75 Claudius Marcellus praises a soldier of wavering loyalty: 216 B.C. Cf. Livy XXIII.15-16; Plut. Marcel. 10-11. Variations of this stratagem and its author are found in IV.VII.36, Plut. Fab. 20 and Val. Max. VII.III.7.

76 Hamilcar's false deserters: 260-241 B.C.

77 Hanno gets rid of troublemakers ("let's you and him fight"): 261 B.C. Cf. Diodor. XXIII.VIII.3. Zonar. VIII.10 attributes this stratagem to Hamilcar.

78 Diodotus gets rid of troublemakers: 168 B.C. In Livy XLIV.44, the author of the stratagem is called Diodorus.

79 the Romans kill an incautious Hasdrubal in front of Panormus: 251 B.C. Cf. Polyb. I.40.

80 Aemilius Paulus' campaign of attrition: 181 B.C. Cf. Livy XL.25, 27-28.

81 Livius' feint: 212-209 B.C.

82 Pompey's sally: 48 B.C. Cf. Caes. B.C. iii.65-70.

83 Flavius Fimbria looks defensive: 85 B.C.

84 Caesar's camp, small and afraid: 54 B.C. Cf. Caes. B. G. V.37-52; Dio XL.10; Polyaen. VIII.XXIII.7.

85 Titurius Sabinus' deception: 56 B.C. Cf. Caes. B. G. III.17-19.

86 noone here but the aged and infirm: 90 B.C.

87 the Numantines' deception: 138 B.C.

88 The Romans are confident: 211 B.C. Cf. Livy XXVI.11; Val. Max. III.VII.10.

89 The Romans mandate by law the taking of Capua: 211 B.C. Cf. Livy XXVI.I.7-8.

Book IV

Having, by extensive reading, collected examples of stratagems, and having arranged these at no small pains, in order to fulfil the promise of my three books (if only I have fulfilled it), in the present book I shall set forth those instances which seemed to fall less naturally under the former classification (which was limited to special types), and which are illustrations rather of military science in general than of stratagems. Inasmuch as these incidents, though famous, belong to a different subject,1 I have given them separate treatment, for fear that if any persons should happen in reading to run across some of them, they might be led by the resemblance to imagine that these examples had been overlooked by me. As supplementary material, of course, these topics called for treatment. In presenting them, I shall endeavour to observe the following categories:

I. On discipline.
II. On the effect of discipline.
III. On restraint and disinterestedness.
IV. On justice.
V. On determination ("the will to victory").
VI. On good will and moderation.
VII.   On sundry maxims and devices.

I. On Discipline

1 When the Roman army before Numantia had become demoralized by the slackness of previous commanders, Publius Scipio reformed it by dismissing an enormous number of camp-followers and by bringing the soldiers to a sense of responsibility through regular daily routine. On the occasion of the frequent marches which he enjoined upon them, he commanded them to carry several days' rations, under such conditions that they became accustomed to enduring cold and rain, and to the fording of streams. Often the general reproached them with timidity and indolence; often he broke utensils which served only the purpose of self-indulgence and were quite unnecessary for campaigning. A notable instance of this severity occurred in the case of the tribune Gaius Memmius, to whom Scipio is said to have exclaimed: "To me you will be worthless merely for a certain period; to yourself and the state forever!"2

2 Quintus Metellus, in the Jugurthine War,3 when discipline had similarly lapsed, restored it by a like severity, while in addition he had forbidden the soldiers to use meat, except when baked or boiled.4

3 Pyrrhus is said to have remarked to his recruiting officer: "You pick out the big men! I'll make them brave."

4 In the consulship of Lucius Paulus and Gaius Varro, soldiers were for the first time compelled to take the ius iurandum. Up to that time the sacramentum was the oath of allegiance administered to them by the tribunes, but they used to pledge each other not to quit the force by flight, or in consequence of fear, and not to leave the ranks except to seek a weapon, strike a foe, or save a comrade.5

5 Scipio Africanus, noticing the shield of a certain soldier rather elaborately decorated, said he didn't wonder the man had adopted it with such care, seeing that he put more trust in it than in his sword.6

6 When Philip was organizing his first army, he forbade anyone to use a carriage. The cavalrymen he permitted to have but one attendant apiece. In the infantry he allowed for every ten men only one servant, who was detailed to carry the mills and ropes.7 When the troops marched out to summer quarters, he commanded each man to carry on his shoulders flour for thirty days.

7 For the purpose of limiting the number of pack animals, by which the march of the army was especially hampered, Gaius Marius had his soldiers fasten their utensils and food up in bundles and hang these on forked poles, to make the burden easy and to facilitate rest; whence the expression "Marius's mules."8

8 When Theagenes, the Athenian, was leading his troops towards Megara and his men inquired as to their place in the ranks, he told them he would assign them their places when they arrived at their destination. Then he secretly sent the cavalry ahead and commanded them, in the guise of enemies, to turn back and attack their comrades. When this plan was carried out and the men whom he had with him made preparations for an encounter with the foe, he permitted the battle-line to be drawn up in such a way that a man took his place where he wished, the most cowardly retiring to the rear, the bravest rushing to the front. He thereupon assigned to each man, for the campaign, the same position in which he had found him.9

9 Lysander, the Spartan, once flogged a soldier who had left the ranks while on the march. When the man said that he had not left the line for the purpose of pillage, Lysander retorted, "I won't have you look as if you were going to pillage."

10 Antigonus, hearing that his son had taken lodgings at the house of a woman who had three handsome daughters, said: "I hear, son, that your lodgings are cramped, owing to the number of mistresses in charge of your house. Get roomier quarters." Having commanded his son to move, he issued an edict that no one under fifty years of age should take lodgings with the mother of a family.10

11 The consul Quintus Metellus, although not prevented by law from having his son with him as a regular tent-mate, yet preferred to have him serve in the ranks.11

12 The consul Publius Rutilius, though he might by law have kept his son in his own tent, made him a soldier in the legion.12

13 Marcus Scaurus forbade his son to come into his presence, since he had retreated before the enemy in the Tridentine Pass. Overwhelmed by the shame of this disgrace, the young man committed suicide.13

14 In ancient times the Romans and other peoples used to make their camps like groups of Punic huts, distributing the troops here and there by cohorts, since the men of old were not acquainted with walls except in the case of cities. Pyrrhus, king of the Epirotes, was the first to inaugurate the custom of concentrating an entire army within the precincts of the same entrenchments. Later the Romans, after defeating Pyrrhus on the Arusian Plains near the city of Maleventum,14 captured his camp, and, noting its plan, gradually came to the arrangement which is in vogue to-day.15

15 At one time, when Publius Nasica was in winter-quarters, although he had no need of ships, yet he determined to construct them, in order that his troops might not become demoralized by idleness, or inflict harm on their allies in consequence of the licence resulting from leisure.16

16 Marcus Cato has handed down the story that, when soldiers were caught in theft, their right hands used to be cut off in the presence of their comrades; or if the authorities wished to impose a lighter sentence, the offender was bled at headquarters.17

17 The Spartan general Clearchus used to tell his troops that their commander ought to be feared more than the enemy, meaning that the death they feared in battle was doubtful, but that execution for desertion was certain.18

18 On motion of Appius Claudius the Senate degraded to the status of foot-soldiers those knights who had been captured and afterwards sent back by Pyrrhus, king of the Epirotes, while the foot-soldiers were degraded to the status of light-armed troops, all being commanded to tent outside the fortifications of the camp until each man should bring in the spoils of two foemen.19

19 The consul Otacilius Crassus ordered those who had been sent under the yoke by Hannibal and had p277then returned, to camp outside the entrenchments, in order that they might become used to dangers while without defences, and so grow more daring against the enemy.20

20 In the consulship of Publius Cornelius Nasica and Decimus Junius those who had deserted from the army were condemned to be scourged publicly with rods and then to be sold into slavery.21

21 Domitius Corbulo, when in Armenia, ordered two squadrons and three cohorts, which had given way before the enemy near the fortress of Initia, to camp outside the entrenchments, until by steady work and successful raids they should atone for their disgrace.22

22 When the consul Aurelius Cotta under pressing necessity ordered the knights to participate in a certain work and a part of them renounced his authority, he made complaint before the censors and had the mutineers degraded. Then from the senators he secured an enactment that arrears of their wages should not be paid. The tribunes of the plebs also carried through a bill with the people on the same matter, so that discipline was maintained by the joint action of all.23

23 When Quintus Metellus Macedonicus was campaigning in Spain, and five cohorts on one occasion had given way before the enemy, he commanded the soldiers to make their wills, and then sent them back to recover the lost ground, threatening that they should not be received in camp except after victory.24

24 The Senate ordered the consul Publius Valerius to lead the army, which had been defeated near the river Siris, to Saepinum, to construct a camp there, and to spend the winter under canvas.25

24a When his soldiers had been disgracefully routed the Senate ordered that no reinforcements should be sent them, unless . . .

25 The legions which had refused to serve in the Punic War26 were sent into a kind of banishment in Sicily, and by vote of the Senate were put on barley rations for seven years.27

26 Because Gaius Titius, commander of a cohort, had given way before some runaway slaves, Lucius Piso ordered him to stand daily in the headquarters of the camp, barefooted, with the

belt of his toga cut and his tunic ungirt, and wait till the night-watchmen came. He also commanded that the culprit should forgo banquets and baths.28

27 Sulla ordered a cohort and its centurions, though whose defences the enemy had broken, to stand continuously at headquarters, wearing helmets and without uniforms.

28 When Domitius Corbulo was campaigning in Armenia, a certain Aemilius Rufus, a praefect of cavalry, gave way before the enemy. On discovering that Rufus had kept his squadron inadequately equipped with weapons, Corbulo directed the lictors to strip the clothes from his back, and ordered the culprit to stand at headquarters in this unseemly plight until he should be released.29

29 When Atilius Regulus was crossing from Samnium to Luceria and his troops turned away from the enemy whom they had encountered, Regulus blocked their retreat with a cohort, as they fled, and ordered them to be cut to pieces as deserters.30

30 The consul Cotta, when in Sicily, flogged a certain Valerius, a noble military tribune belonging to the Valerian gens.31

31 The same Cotta, when about to cross over to Messana to take the auspices afresh, placed in charge of the blockade of the Liparian Islands a ceremony Publius Aurelius, who was connected with him by ties of blood. But when Aurelius's line of works was burned and his camp captured, Cotta had him scourged with rods and ordered him to be reduced to the ranks and to perform the tasks of a common soldier.32

32 The censor Fulvius Flaccus removed from the Senate his own brother Fulvius, because the latter without the command of the consul had disbanded the legion in which he was tribune of the soldiers.33

33 On one occasion when Marcus Cato, who had lingered for several days on a hostile shore, had at length set sail, after three times giving the signal for departure, and a certain soldier, who had been left behind, with cries and gestures from the land, begged to be picked up, Cato turned his whole fleet back to the shore, arrested the man, and commanded him to be put to death, thus preferring to make an example of the fellow than to have him ignominiously put to death by the enemy.34

34 In the case of those who quitted their places in the line, Appius Claudius picked out every tenth man by lot and had him clubbed to death.

35 In the case of two legions which had given way before the foe, the consul Fabius Rullus chose men by lot and beheaded them in the sight of their comrades.

36 Aquilius beheaded three men from each of the centuries whose position had been broken through by the enemy.

37 Marcus Antonius, when fire had been set to his line of works by the enemy, decimated the soldiers of two cohorts of those who were on the works, and punished the centurions of each cohort. Besides this, he dismissed the commanding officer in disgrace, and ordered the rest of the legion to be put on barley rations.35

38 The legion which had plundered the city of Rhegium without the orders of its commander was punished as follows: four thousand men were put under guard and executed. Moreover the Senate by decree made it a crime to bury any one of these or indulge in mourning for them.36

39 The dictator Lucius Papirius Cursor demanded that Fabius Rullus, his master of the horse, be scourged, and was on the point of beheading him, because he had engaged in battle against orders — successfully withal. Even in the face of the efforts and please of the soldiers, Papirius refused to renounce his purpose of punishment, actually following Rullus, when he fled for refuge to Rome, and not even there abandoning his threats of execution until Fabius and his father fell at the knees of Papirius, and the Senate and people alike joined in their petition.37

40 Manlius, to whom the name "The Masterful" was afterwards given, had his own son scourged and beheaded in the sight of the army, because, even though he came out victorious, he had engaged in battle with the enemy contrary to the orders of his father.38

41 The younger Manlius, when the army was preparing to mutiny in his behalf against his father, said that no one was of such importance that discipline will be destroyed on his account, and so induced his comrades to suffer him to be punished.38

42 Quintus Fabius Maximus cut off the right hands of deserters.39

43 When the consul Gaius Curio was campaigning near Dyrrhachium in the war against the Dardani,40 and one of the five legions, having mutinied, had refused service and declared it would not follow his rash leadership on a difficult and dangerous enterprise, he led out four legions in arms and ordered them to take their stand in the ranks with weapons drawn, as if in battle. Then he commanded the mutinous legion to advance without arms, and forced its members to strip for work and cut straw under the eyes of armed guards. The following day, in like manner, he compelled them to strip and dig ditches, and by no entreaties of the legion could he be induced to renounce his purpose of withdrawing its standards, abolishing its name, and distributing its members to fill out other legions.

44 In the consulship of Quintus Fulvius and Appius Claudius, the soldiers, who after the battle of Cannae had been banished to Sicily by the Senate, petitioned the consul Marcellus to be led to battle. Marcellus consulted the Senate, who declared it was not their pleasure that the public welfare should be trusted to those who had proved disloyal. Yet they empowered Marcellus to do what seemed best to him, provided none of the soldiers should be relieved of duty, honoured with a gift or reward, or conveyed back to Italy, so long as there were any Carthaginians in the country.41

45 Marcus Salinator, when ex-consul, was condemned by the people because he had not divided the booty equally among his soldiers.42

46 When the consul Quintus Petilius had been killed in battle by the Ligurians, the Senate decreed that that legion in whose ranks the consul had been slain should, as a whole, be reported "deficient";43 that its year's pay should be withheld, and its wages reduced.44

II. On the Effect of Discipline

1 When, during the Civil War, the armies of Brutus and Cassius were marching together through Macedonia, the story goes that the army of Brutus arrived first at a stream which had

to be bridged, but that the troops of Cassius were the first in constructing the bridge and in effecting a passage. This rigorous discipline made Cassius's men superior to those of Brutus not only in constructing military works, but also in the general conduct of the war.45

2 When Gaius Marius had the option of choosing a force from two armies, one of which had served under Rutilius, the other under Metellus and later under himself, he preferred the troops of Rutilius, though fewer in number, because he deemed them of trustier discipline.46

3 By improving discipline, Domitius Corbulo withstood the Parthians with a force of only two legions and a very few auxiliaries.47

4 Alexander of Macedon conquered the world, in the face of innumerable forces of enemies, by means of forty thousand men long accustomed to discipline under his father Philip.48

5 Cyrus in his war against the Persians overcame incalculable difficulties with a force of only fourteen thousand armed men.49

6 With four thousand men, of whom only four hundred were cavalry, Epaminondas, the Theban leader, conquered a Spartan army of twenty-four thousand infantry and sixteen hundred cavalry.50

7 A hundred thousand barbarians were defeated in battle by fourteen thousand Greeks, the number assisting Cyrus against Artaxerxes.51

8 The same fourteen thousand Greeks, having lost their generals in battle, returned unharmed through difficult and unknown places, having committed the management of their retreat to one of their number, Xenophon, the Athenian.52

9 When Xerxes was defied by the three hundred Spartans at Thermopylae and had with difficulty destroyed them, he declared that he had been deceived, because, while he had numbers enough, yet of real men who adhered to discipline he had none.53

III. On Restraint and Disinterestedness

1 The story goes that Marcus Cato was content with the same wine as the men of his crews.54

2 When Cineas, ambassador of the Epirotes, offered Fabricius a large amount of gold, the latter rejected it, declaring that he preferred to rule those who had gold rather than to have it himself.55

3 Atilius Regulus, though he had been in charge of the greatest enterprises, was so poor that he supported himself, his wife, and children on a small farm which was tilled by a single steward. Hearing of the death of this steward, Regulus wrote to the Senate requesting them to appoint someone to succeed him in the command, since his property was left in jeopardy by the death of his slave, and his own presence at home was necessary.56

4 Gnaeus Scipio, after successful exploits in Spain, died in the extremest poverty, not even leaving money enough for a dowry for his daughters. The Senate, therefore, in consequence of their poverty, furnished them dowries at public expense.57

5 The Athenians did the same thing for the daughters of Aristides, who died in the greatest poverty after directing the most important enterprises.58

6 Epaminondas, the Theban general, was a man of such simple habits that among his belongings nothing was found beyond a mat and a single spit.59

7 Hannibal was accustomed to rise while it was still dark, but never took any rest before night. At dusk, and not before, he called his friends to dinner; and not more than two couches60 were ever filled with dinner guests at his headquarters.61

8 The same general, when serving under Hasdrubal as commander, usually slept on the bare ground, wrapped only in a common military cloak.61

8 The story goes that Scipio Aemilianus used to eat bread offered him as he walked along on the march in the company of his friends.

10 The same story is related of Alexander of Macedon.

11 We read that Masinissa, when in his ninetieth year, used to eat at noon, standing or walking about in front of his tent.62

12 When, in honour of his defeat of the Sabines, the Senate offered Manius Curius a larger amount of ground than the discharged troops were receiving, he was content with the allotment of ordinary soldiers, declaring that that man was a bad citizen who was not satisfied with what the rest received.63

13 The restraint of an entire army was also often noteworthy, as for example of the troops which served under Marcus Scaurus. For Scaurus has left it on record that a tree laden with fruit, at the far end of the fortified enclosure of the camp, was found, the day after the withdrawal of the army, with the fruit undisturbed.64

14 In the war waged under the auspices of the Emperor Caesar Domitianus Augustus Germanicus and begun by Julius Civilis in Gaul, the very wealthy city of the Lingones,a which had revolted to Civilis, feared that it would be plundered by the approaching army of Caesar. But when, contrary to expectation, the inhabitants remained unharmed and lost none of their property, they returned to their loyalty, and handed over to meb seventy thousand armed men.65

15 After the capture of Corinth, Lucius Mummius adorned not merely Italy, but also the provinces, with statues and paintings. Yet he refrained so scrupulously from appropriating anything from such vast spoils to his own use that his daughter was in actual need and the Senate furnished her dowry at the public expense.66

IV. On Justice

1 When Camillus was besieging the Faliscans, a school teacher took the sons of the Faliscans outside the walls, as though for a walk, and then delivered them up, saying that, if they should be retained as hostages, the city would be forced to execute the orders of Camillus. But Camillus not only spurned the teacher's perfidy, but tying his hands behind his back, turned him over to the boys to be driven back to their parents with switches. He thus gained by kindness a victory which he had scorned to secure by fraud; for the Faliscans, in consequence of this act of justice, voluntarily surrendered to him.67

2 The physician of Pyrrhus, king of the Epirotes, came to Fabricius, general of the Romans, and promised to give Pyrrhus poison if an adequate reward should be guaranteed him for the

service. Fabricius, not considering that victory called for any such crime, exposed the physician to the king, and by this honourable act succeeded in inducing Pyrrhus to seek the friendship of the Romans.68

V. On Determination ("The Will to Victory")

1 When the soldiers of Gnaeus Pompey threatened to plunder the money which was being carried for the triumph, Servilius and Glaucia urged him to distribute it among the troops, in order to avoid the outbreak of a mutiny. Thereupon Pompey declared he would forgo a triumph, and would die rather than yield to the insubordination of his soldiers; and after upbraiding them in vehement language, he threw in their faces the fasces wreathed with laurel, that they might start their plundering by seizing these. Through the odium thus aroused he reduced his men to obedience.69

2 When a sedition broke out in the tumult of the Civil War, and feeling ran especially high, Gaius Caesar dismissed from service an entire legion, and beheaded the leaders of the mutiny. Later, when the very men he had dismissed entreated him to remove their disgrace, he restored them and had in them the very best soldiers.70

3 Postumius, when ex-consul, having appealed to the courage of his troops, and having been asked by them what commands he gave, told them to imitate him. Thereupon he seized a standard and led the attack on the enemy. His soldiers followed and won the victory.

4 Claudius Marcellus, having unexpectedly come upon some Gallic troops, turned his horse about in a circle, looking around for a way of escape. Seeing danger on every hand, with a prayer to the gods, he broke into the midst of the enemy. By his amazing audacity he threw them into consternation, slew their leader,71 and actually carried away the spolia opima72 in a situation where there had scarcely remained a hope of saving his life.73

5 Lucius Paulus, after the loss of his army at Cannae, being offered a horse by Lentulus with which to effect his escape, refused to survive the disaster, although it had not been occasioned by him, and remained seated on the rock against which he had leaned when wounded, until he was overpowered and stabbed by the enemy.74

6 Paulus's colleague, Varro, showed even greater resolution in continuing alive after the same disaster, and the Senate and the people thanked him "because," they said, "he did not despair of the commonwealth." But throughout the rest of his life he gave proof that he had remained alive not from desire of life, but because of his love of country. He suffered his beard and hair to remain untrimmed, and never afterwards reclined when he took food at table. Even when honours were decreed him by the people he declined them, saying that State needed more fortunate magistrates than himself.75

7 After the complete rout of the Romans at Cannae, when Sempronius Tuditanus and Gnaeus Octavius, tribunes of the soldiers, were besieged in the smaller camp,76 they urged their comrades to draw their swords and accompany them in a dash through the forces of the enemy, declaring that they themselves were resolved on this course, even if no one else possessed the courage to break through. Although among the wavering crowd only twelve knights and fifty foot-soldiers were found who had the courage to accompany them, yet they reached Canusium unscathed.77

8 When Gaius Fonteius Crassus was in Spain, he set out with three thousand men on a foraging expedition and was enveloped in an awkward position by Hasdrubal. In the early part

of the night, at a time when such a thing was least expected, having communicated his purpose only to the centurions of the first rank, he broke through the pickets of the enemy.

9 When the consul Cornelius had been caught in an awkward position by the enemy in the Samnite War, Publius Decius, tribune of the soldiers, urged him to send a small force to occupy a neighbouring hill, and volunteered to act as leader of those who should be sent. The enemy, thus diverted to a different quarter, allowed the consul to escape, but surrounded Decius and besieged him. Decius, however, extricated himself from this predicament also by making a sortie at night, and escaped unharmed along with his men and rejoined the consul.78

10 Under the consul Atilius Calatinus the same thing was done by a man whose name is variously reported. Some say he was called Laberius, and some Quintus Caedicius, but most give it as Calpurnius Flamma. This man, seeing that the army had entered a valley, the sides and all commanding parts of which the enemy had occupied, asked and received from the consul three hundred soldiers. After exhorting these to save the army by their valour, he hastened to the centre of the valley. To crush him and his followers, the enemy descended from all quarters, but, being held in check in a long and fierce battle, they thus afforded the consul an opportunity of extricating his army.79

11 Gaius Caesar, when about to fight the Germans and their king Ariovistus, at a time when his own men had been thrown into panic, called his soldiers together and declared to the assembly that on that day he proposed to employ the services of the tenth legion alone. In this way he caused the soldiers of this legion to be stirred by his tribute to their unique heroism, while the rest were overwhelmed with mortification to think that reputation for courage should be confined to others.80

12 A certain Spartan noble, when Philip declared he p303would cut them off from many things, unless the state surrendered to him, asked: "He won't cut us off from dying in defence of our country, will he?"81

13 Leonidas, the Spartan, in reply to the statement that the Persians would create clouds by the multitude of their arrows, is reported to have said: "We shall fight all the better in the shade."82

14 When Gaius Aelius, a city praetor, was holding court on one occasion, a woodpecker lighted upon his head. The soothsayers were consulted and made answer that, if the bird should be allowed to go, the victory would fall to the enemy, but that, if it were killed, the Roman people would prevail, though Gaius and all his house should perish. Aelius, however, did not hesitate to kill the woodpecker. Our army won the day, but Aelius himself, with fourteen others of the same family, was slain in battle. Certain authorities do not believe that the man referred to was Gaius Caelius, but a certain Laelius, and that they were Laelii, not Caelii, who perished.83

15 Two Romans bearing the name Publius Decius, first the father, later the son, sacrificed their lives to save the State during their tenure of office. By spurring their horses against the foe they won victory for their country.84

16 When waging war against Aristonicus in Asia somewhere between Elaea and Myrina, Publius Crassus fell into the hands of the enemy and was being led away alive. Scorning the thought of captivity for a Roman consul, he used the stick, with which he had urged on his horse, to gouge out the eye of the Thracian by whom he was held captive. The Thracian,

infuriated with the pain, stabbed him to death. Thus, as he desired, Crassus escaped the disgrace of servitude.85

17 Marcus, son of Cato the Censor, in a certain battle fell off his horse, which had stumbled. Cato picked himself up, but noticing that his sword had slipped out of its scabbard and fearing disgrace, went back among the enemy, and though he received a number of wounds, finally recovered his sword and made his way back to his comrades.86

18 The inhabitants of Petelia, when they were blockaded by the Carthaginians, sent away the children and the aged, on account of the shortage of food. They themselves, supporting life on hides, moistened and then dried by the fire, on leaves of trees, and on all sorts of animals, sustained the siege for eleven months.87

19 The Spaniards, when blockaded at Consabra, endured all these same hardships; nor did they surrender the town to Hirtuleius.88

20 The story goes that the inhabitants of Casilinum, when blockaded by Hannibal, suffered such shortage of food that a mouse was sold for two hundred denarii,89 and that the man who sold it died of starvation, while the purchaser lived. Yet the inhabitants persisted in maintaining their loyalty to the Romans.90

21 When Mithridates was besieging Cyzicus, he paraded the captives from that city and exhibited them to the besieged, thinking thus to force the people of the town to surrender, through compassion for their fellows. But the townspeople urged the prisoners to meet death with heroism, and persisted in maintaining their loyalty to the Romans.91

22 The inhabitants of Segovia, when Viriathus proposed to send them back their wives and children, preferred to witness the execution of their loved ones rather than to fail the Romans.92

23 The inhabitants of Numantia preferred to lock the doors of their houses and die of hunger rather than surrender.93

VI. On Good Will and Moderation

1 Quintus Fabius,94 upon being urged by his son to seize an advantageous position at the expense of losing a few men, asked: "Do you want to be one of those few?"

2 When Xenophon on one occasion happened to be on horseback and had just ordered the infantry to take possession of a certain eminence, he heard one of the soldiers muttering that it was an easy matter for a mounted man to order such difficult enterprises. At this Xenophon leaped down and set the man from the ranks on his horse, while he himself hurried on foot with all speed to the eminence he had indicated. The soldier, unable to endure the shame of this performance, voluntarily dismounted amid the jeers of his comrades. It was with difficulty, however, that the united efforts of the troops induced Xenophon to mount his horse and to restrict his energies to the duties which devolved upon a commander.95

3 When Alexander was marching at the head of his troops one winter's day, he sat down by a fire and began to review the troops as they passed by. Noticing a certain soldier who was almost dead with the cold, he bade him sit in his place, adding: "If you had been born among the Persians, it would be a capital crime for you to sit on the king's seat; but since you were born in Macedonia, that privilege is yours.96

4 When the Deified Vespasianus Augustus learned that a certain youth, of good birth, but ill adapted to military service, had received a high appointment because of his straitened circumstances, Vespasian settled a sum of money on him, and gave him an honourable discharge.

VII. On Sundry Maxims and Devices

1 Gaius Caesar used to say that he followed the same policy towards the enemy as did many doctors when dealing with the physical ailments, namely, that of conquering the foe by hunger rather than by steel.97

2 Domitius Corbulo used to say that the pick was the weapon with which to beat the enemy.

3 Lucius Paulus used to say that a general ought to be an old man in character, meaning thereby that moderate counsels should be followed.98

4 When people said of Scipio Africanus that he lacked aggressiveness, he is reported to have answered: "My mother bore me a general, not a warrior."

5 When a Teuton challenged Gaius Marius and called upon him to come forth, Marius answered that, if the man was desirous of death, he could end his life with a halter. Then, when the fellow persisted, Marius confronted him with a gladiator of despicable size, whose life was almost spent, and told the Teuton that, if he would first defeat this gladiator, he himself would then fight with him.

6 After Quintus Sertorius had learned by experience that he was by no means a match for the whole Roman army, and wished to prove this to the barbarians also, who were rashly demanding battle, he brought into their presence two horses, one very strong, the other very feeble. Then he brought up two youths of corresponding physique, one robust, the other slight. The stronger youth was commanded to pull out the entire tail of the feeble horse, while the slight youth was commanded to pull out the hairs of the strong horse, one by one. Then, when the slight youth had succeeded in his task, while the strong one was still struggling vainly with the tail of the weak horse, Sertorius observed: "By this illustration I have exhibited to you, my men, the nature of the Roman cohorts. They are invincible to him who attacks them in a body; yet he who assails them by groups will tear and rend them."99

7 The consul Valerius Laevinus, having caught a spy within his camp, and having entire confidence in his own forces, ordered the man to be led around, observing that, for the sake of terrifying the enemy, his army was open to inspection by the spies of the enemy, as often as they wished.100

8 Caedicius, a centurion of the first rank, who acted as leader in Germany, when, after the Varian disaster,101 our men were beleaguered,° was afraid that the barbarians would bring up to the fortifications the wood which they had gathered, and would set fire to his camp. He therefore pretended to be in need of fuel, and sent out men in every direction to steal it. In this way he caused the Germans to remove the whole supply of felled trees.102

9 Gnaeus Scipio, in a naval combat, hurled jars filled with pitch and rosin among the vessels of the enemy, in order that damage might result both from the weight of the missiles and from the scattering of their contents, which would serve as fuel for a conflagration.

10 Hannibal suggested to King Antiochus that he hurl jars filled with vipers among the ships of the enemy, in order that the crews, through fear of these, might be kept from fighting and from performing their nautical duties.103

11 Prusias did the same, when his fleet was by now giving way.104

12 Marcus Porcius Cato, having boarded the ships of the enemy, drove from them the Carthaginians. Then, having distributed their weapons and insignia among his own men, he sank many ships of the enemy, deceiving them by their own equipment.

13 Inasmuch as the Athenians had been subject to repeated attacks by the Spartans, on one occasion, in the course of a festival which they were celebrating outside the city in honour of Minerva, they studiously affected the role of worshippers, yet with weapons concealed beneath their clothing. When the ceremonial was over, they did not immediately return to Athens, but at once marched swiftly upon Sparta at a time when they were least feared, and themselves devastated the lands of an enemy whose victims they had often been.

14 Cassius set fire to some transports which were of no great use for anything else, and sent them with a fair wind against the fleet of the enemy, thereby destroying it by fire.104

15 When Marcus Livius had routed Hasdrubal, and certain persons urged him to pursue the enemy to annihilation, he answered: "Let some survive to carry to the enemy the tidings of our victory!"105

16 Scipio Africanus used to say that a road not only ought to be afforded the enemy for flight, but that it ought even to be paved.106

17 Paches, the Athenian, on one occasion declared that the enemy would be spared, if they put aside the steel. When they had all complied with these terms, he ordered the entire number to be executed, since they had steel brooches on their cloaks.107

18 When Hasdrubal had invaded the territory of the Numidians for the purpose of subduing them, and they were preparing to resist, he declared that he had come to capture elephants, an animal in which Numidia abounds. For this privilege they demanded money, and Hasdrubal promised to pay it. Having by these representations thrown them off the scent, he attacked them and brought them under his power.

19 Alcetas, the Spartan, in order the more easily to make a surprise attack on a supply convoy of the Thebans, got ready his ships in a secret place, and exercised his rowers by turns on a single galley, as though that was all he had. Then at a certain time, as the Theban vessels were sailing past, he sent all his ships against them and captured their supplies.108

20 When Ptolemy with a weak force was contending against Perdiccas's powerful army, he arranged for a few horsemen to drive along animals of all sorts, with brush fastened to their backs for them to trail behind them. He himself went ahead with the forces which he had. As a consequence, the dust raised by the animals produced the appearance of a mighty army following, and the enemy, terrified by this impression, were defeated.109

21 Myronides, the Athenian, when about to fight on an open plain against the Thebans, who were very strong in cavalry, warned his troops that, if they stood their ground, there was some hope of safety, but that, if they gave way, destruction was absolutely certain. In this way he encouraged his men and won the victory.110

22 When Gaius Pinarius was in charge of the garrison of Henna in Sicily, the magistrates of the city demanded the keys of the gates, which he had in his keeping. Suspecting that they were preparing to go over to the Carthaginians, he asked for the space of a single night to consider the matter; and, revealing to his soldiers the treachery of the Greeks, he instructed them to get ready and wait for his signal on the morrow. At daybreak, in the presence of his troops, he announced to the people of Henna that he would surrender the keys, if all the inhabitants of the town should be agreed in their view. When the entire populace assembled in the theatre to settle this matter, and, with the obvious purpose of revolting, made the same demand, Pinarius gave the signal to his soldiers and murdered all the people of Henna.111

23 Iphicrates, the Athenian general, once rigged up his own fleet after the style of the enemy, and sailed away to a certain city whose people he viewed with suspicion. Being welcomed with unrestrained enthusiasm, he thus discovered their treachery and sacked their town.112

24 When Tiberius Gracchus had proclaimed that he would confer freedom on such of the volunteer slaves as showed courage, but would crucify the cowards, some four thousand men who had fought rather listlessly, gathered on a fortified hill in fear of punishment. Thereupon Gracchus sent men to tell them that in his opinion the whole force of volunteer slaves had shared in the victory, since they had routed the enemy. By this expression of confidence he freed them from their apprehensions and took them back again.113

25 After the battle of Lake Trasimenus, where the Romans suffered great disaster, Hannibal, having brought six thousand of the enemy under his power by virtue of a covenant he had made, generously allowed the allies of the "Latin Name"114 to return to their cities, declaring that he was waging war for the purpose of freeing Italy. As a result, by means of their assistance he received in surrender a number of tribes.115

26 When Locri was blockaded by Crispinus, admiral of our fleet, Mago spread the rumour in the Roman camp that Hannibal had slain Marcellus and was coming to relieve Locri from blockade. Then, secretly sending out cavalry, he commanded them to show themselves on the mountains, which were in view. By doing this, he caused Crispinus, in the belief that Hannibal was at hand, to board his vessels and make off.116

27 Scipio Aemilianus, in the operations before Numantia, distributed archers and slingers not only among all his cohorts, but even among all the centuries.117

28 When Pelopidas, the Theban, had been put to flight by the Thessalians and had crossed the river over which he had constructed an emergency bridge, he ordered his rearguard to burn the bridge, in order that it might not serve also as a means of passage to the enemy who were following him.118

29 When the Romans in certain operations were no match for the Campanian cavalry, Quintus Naevius, a centurion in the army of Fulvius Flaccus, the proconsul, conceived the plan of picking from the whole army the men who seemed swiftest of foot and of medium stature, arming them with small shields, helmets, and swords, and giving to each man seven spears, •about four feet in length. These men he attached to the cavalry, and commanded them to advance to the very walls, and then, taking their position at that point, to fight amid the cavalry of the enemy, when our cavalry retreated. By this means the Campanians suffered severely, and especially their horses. When these were thrown into confusion, victory became easy for our troops.119

30 When Publius Scipio was in Lydia, and observed that the army of Antiochus was demoralized by the rain, which fell day and night without cessation, and when he further noted that not only were men and horses exhausted, but that even the bows were rendered useless from the effect of the dampness on their strings, he urged his brother to engage in battle on the following day, although it was consecrated to religious observance. The adoption of this plan was followed by victory.120

31 When Cato was ravaging Spain, the envoys of the Ilergetes, a tribe allied with the Romans, came to him and begged for assistance. Cato, unwilling either to alienate his allies by refusing aid, or to diminish his own strength by dividing his forces, ordered a third part of his soldiers to prepare rations and embark on their ships, directing them to return and to allege head winds as the reason for this action. Meanwhile the report of approaching aid went on before them, raising the hopes of the Ilergetes, and shattering the plans of the enemy.121

32 Since in the army of Pompey there was a large force of Roman cavalry, which by its skill in arms wrought havoc among the soldiers of Gaius Caesar, the latter ordered his troops to aim with their swords at the faces and eyes of the enemy. He thus forced the enemy to avert their faces and retire.122

33 When the Voccaei were hard pressed by Sempronius Gracchus in a pitched battle, they surrounded their entire force with a ring of carts, which they had filled with their bravest warriors dressed in women's clothes. Sempronius rose up with greater daring to assault the enemy, because he imagined himself proceeding against women, whereupon those in the carts attacked him and put him to flight.123

34 When Eumenes of Cardia, one of the successors of Alexander, was besieged in a certain stronghold, and was unable to exercise his horses, he had them suspended during certain hours each day in such a position that, resting on their hind legs and with their fore feet in the air, they moved their legs till the sweat ran, in their efforts to regain their natural posture.124

35 When certain barbarians promised Marcus Cato guides for the march and also reinforcements, provided that a large sum of money should be assured them, he did not hesitate to make the promise, since, if they won, he could reward them from the spoils of the enemy, while, if they were slain, he would be released from his pledge.125

36 When a certain Statilius, a knight of distinguished record, evinced an inclination to desert to the enemy, Quintus Maximus ordered him to be summoned to his presence, and apologized for not having known until then the real merits of Statilius, owing to the jealousy of his fellow-soldiers. Then, giving Statilius a horse and bestowing a large gift of money besides, he succeeded in sending away rejoicing a man who, when summoned, was conscience-stricken; he succeeded also in securing for the future a loyal and brave knight in place of one whose fealty was in doubt.126

37 Philip,127 having heard that a certain Pythias, an excellent warrior, had become estranged from him because he was too poor to support his three daughters, and was not assisted by the king, and having been warned by certain persons to be on his guard against the man, replied: "What! If part of my body were diseased, should I cut it off, rather than give it treatment?" Then, quietly drawing Pythias aside for a confidential talk, and learning the seriousness of his domestic embarrassments, he supplied him with funds, and found in him a better and more devoted adherent than before the estrangement.

38 After an unsuccessful battle with the Carthaginians, in which he had lost his colleague Marcellus, Titius Quinctius Crispinus, learning that Hannibal had obtained possession of the ring of the slain hero, sent letters among all the municipal towns of Italy, warning the inhabitants to give credit to no letters which should be brought sealed with the ring of Marcellus. As a result of this advice, Salapia and other cities were assailed in vain by Hannibal's insidious efforts.128

39 After the disaster at Cannae, when the Romans were so terror-stricken that a large part of survivors thought of abandoning Italy, and that too with the endorsement of nobles of the highest standing, Publius Scipio, then extremely young, in the very assembly where such a course was being discussed, proclaimed with great vehemence that he would slay with his own hand whoever refused to declare on oath that he cherished no purpose of abandoning the State. Having first bound himself with such an oath, he drew his sword and threatened death to one of those standing near unless he too should take the oath. This man was constrained by fear to swear allegiance; the rest were compelled by the example of the first.129

40 When the camp of the Volscians had been pitched near bushes and woods, Camillus set fire to everything which could carry the flames, once started, up to the very fortifications. In this way he deprived the enemy of their camp.130

41 In the Social War Publius Crassus was cut off in almost the same way with all his troops.131

42 When Quintus Metellus was about to break camp in Spain and wished to keep his soldiers in line, he proclaimed that he had discovered that an ambush had been laid by the enemy; therefore the soldiers should not quit the standards nor break ranks. Though he had done this merely for purposes of discipline, yet happening to meet with an actual ambuscade, he found his soldiers unafraid, since he had given them warning.132

The Editor's Notes:

0 Book IV: On the authenticity of Book IV, see Introduction, pp. xix ff.

1 a different subject: That is, different from the class of stratagems proper.

2 Scipio pares down superfluities: 134 B.C. Cf. Val. Max. II.VII.1; Livy Per. 57; Polyaen. VIII.XVI.2.

3 Metellus in the Jugurthine War: 109 B.C. Cf. Val. Max. II.VII.2; Sall. Jug. 45. Polyaen. VIII.XVI.2 and Plut. Apophth. Scip. Min. 16 attribute this to Scipio.

4 no meat except baked or boiled: The point of the prohibition is not obvious to the modern sense.

5 soldiers required to take the ius iurandum: 216 B.C. Cf. Livy XXII.38. Up to the time of the Battle of Cannae, there were two military oaths, the sacramentum, which was compulsory and was administered by the consul when the soldier first enlisted, and the ius iurandum, a voluntary oath taken before a tribune when the soldiers were assigned to separate divisions. In 216 the two were united, and thereafter the ius iurandum, administered by the military tribune, was compulsory. The facts here stated are slightly at variance with the general understanding.

6 Scipio Africanus and the fancy shield: 134 B.C. Cf. Livy Per. 57; Plut. Apophth. Scip. Min. 18; Polyaen. VIII.XVI.3,4.

7 mills and ropes: The mills were for grinding corn.° The allusion to the ropes is not clear.

8 Marius's mules: Cf. Fest. Paul. 24, 2; 148, 6.

9 Theagenes' place assignments: Polyaen. V.XXVIII.1 attributes this to Theognis; in III.IX.10, he attributes it to Iphicrates.

10 Antigonus' son — cramped lodgings: 323-321 B.C. Cf. Plut. Demetr. 23, Apophth. Antig. 5.

11 Quintus Metellus' son in the field: 143 (?) 109 (?) B.C. Sall. Jug. lxiv.4 says that Metellus Numidicus kept his son with him as tent-mate.

12 Publius Rutilius' son in the field: 105 B.C.

13 Marcus Scaurus' son retreats: 102 B.C. Cf. Val. Max. V.VIII.4.

14 Maleventum: The modern Benevento. Pyrrhus was defeated here in 275 B.C.

15 Pyrrhus and the origin of the Roman castrum: Cf. Livy XXXV.14. Plut. Pyrrh. 16 represents Pyrrhus, on the other hand, marvelling at the arrangement of the Roman camp.

16 Nasica's ships: 194-193 B.C.

17 the offender was bled at headquarters: Gell. X.VIII.1 gives an interesting conjecture as to the origin of this second punishment.

18 Clearchus and the odds of getting killed: 431-401 B.C. Cf. Val. Max. II.VII.extr.2; Xen. Anab. II.VI.10.

19 Appius Claudius degrades captured soldiers: 279 B.C. Cf. Val. Max. II.VII.15; Eutrop. II.13.

20 Otacilius Crassus toughens up his weaker soldiers: Manius Otacilius Crassus was consul in 263 and 246 B.C. Titus Otacilius Crassus was consul in 261 B.C.

21 Nasica and Junius' treatment of deserters: 138 B.C. Cf. Livy Per. 55.

22 Corbulo's treatment of deserters: 58-59 A.D. Cf. Tac. Ann. XIII.36.

23 Cotta's discipline: 252 B.C. Val. Max. II.IX.7 cites a somewhat similar case of discipline.

24 Quintus Metellus Macedonicus — "write your wills, men": 143 B.C. Cf. Val. Max. II.VII.10; Vell. II.5.

25 The Senate orders winter in the field as a disciplinary measure: 280 B.C. Publius Valerius Laevinus.

26 legions refusing to serve in the Punic War: In the Second Punic War, after Cannae.

27 mutinous legions on barley rations: Cf. Liv XXIV.18. The substitution of barley for wheat rations was a common form of punishment; Cf. Suet. Aug. 24; Plut. Marc. 25.

28 Gaius Titius stands in his underwear: 133 B.C. Cf. Val. Max. II.VII.9.

29 Aemilius Rufus stands •nudus: 58-59 A.D.

30 Atilius Regulus' punishment of deserters: 294 B.C. Cf. II.VIII.11 and note.

31 Cotta flogs a young man from a powerful family: 252 B.C.

32 Cotta scourges and demotes a relative: Cf. Val. Max. II.VII.4.

33 Fulvius Flaccus removes his brother from the Senate: 174 B.C. Cf. Val. Max. II.VII.5; Livy XL.41, XLI.27; Vell. I.X.6.

34 Cato puts to death a soldier who had hidden from action: 471 B.C. Cf. Livy II.59; Dionys. IX.50; Zonar. VII.17.

35 Marcus Antonius decimates soldiers: 36 B.C. Cf. Plut. Ant. 39.

36 the plundering legion: When Pyrrhus was in southern Italy, the people of Rhegium applied to Rome for assistance, and the Romans sent them a garrison of four thousand soldiers, levied among the Latin colonies in Campania. In 279 these troops seized the town, killed or expelled the male inhabitants, and took possession of the women and children. Cf. Livy XXVIII.28; Val. Max. II.VII.15; Polyb. I.VII.6-13; Oros. IV.III.3-5.

37 Papirius Cursor has his master of the horse scourged: 325 B.C. Cf. Livy VIII.29 ff.; Val. Max. II.VII.8, III.II.9; Eutr. II.8.

38 Manlius has his son scourged and beheaded; with that kind of father I too would have agreed to it: 340 B.C. Cf. Livy VIII.7; Val. Max. II.VII.6; Sall. Cat. 52; Cic. de Fin. I.VII.23, de Off. III.XXXI.112. The father, Titus Manlius Torquatus, was the son of Lucius Manlius, dictator in 363, who had also received the cognomen Imperiosus on account of his severity.

39 Fabius Maximus' left-handed deserters: 142-140 B.C. Quintus Fabius Maximus Servilianus. Cf. Val. Max. II.VII.11; Oros. V.IV.12.

40 the Dardani: One of the leading tribes of Illyria, subdued by the Romans. According to Livy Per. 92, 95 and Eutrop. VI.2, Curio was proconsul when he carried on this campaign in 75 B.C.

41 Marcellus and the soldiers of Cannae: 212 B.C. Cf. Livy XXV.5-7; Val. Max. II.VII.15; Plut. Marc. 13. Marcellus was proconsul, not consul. Cf. Livy XXVI.1.

42 Marcus Salinator's unequal division of booty: 218 B.C. Cf. Livy XXVII.34, XXIX.37.

43 "deficient": The term infrequens was technically applied to soldiers who were absent from or irregular in attendance on their duties.

44 Quintus Petilius' deficient legion: 176 B.C. Cf. Livy XLI.18; Val. Max. II.VII.15.

45 Technical skill better than raw speed: 42 B.C.

46 Marius prefers disciplined soldiers to his own: 104 B.C.

47 Corbulo's legions — discipline more important than numbers: 55-59 A.D. Cf. Tac. Ann. XIII.8, 35.

48 Alexander's army: 334 B.C. Cf. Livy XXXV.14; Justin. XI.6; Plut. Alex. 15. The numbers vary in the different authors.

49 Cyrus' fourteen thousand men: 401 B.C. Cf. IV.II.7; Xen. Anab. I.II.9; Plut. Artax. 6; Diodor. XIV.XIX.6.

50 Epaminondas' victory despite being outnumbered: 371 B.C. Battle of Leuctra. Diodor. XV.52 ff. and Plut. Pelop. 20 give different numbers.

51 a few thousand disciplined Greeks better than hordes of Persians: Battle of Cunaxa. Cf. IV.II.5.

52 discipline pulls a Greek army thru a long trek across Asia Minor: Cf. Xen. Anab. III.1 ff.

53 Xerxes regrets he had no disciplined men: 480 B.C. In Herod. VII.210, the historian himself, not the king, makes this observation.

54 Cato drank the same wine as his crews: Cf. Val. Max. IV.III.11; Plin. H. N. XIV.3,14.°

55 Fabricius' leveraged assets: 280 B.C. Gell. I.14 tells this story of Fabricius; usually it is related of Curius. Cf. Val. Max. IV.III.5; Cic. de Sen. xvi.55; Plut. Apophth. M'. Curii.

56 poverty and honesty of Atilius Regulus: 255 B.C. Cf. Val. Max. IV.IV.6; Livy Per. 18; Senec. ad Helv. 12; Apul. Apol. 18.

57 poverty and honesty of Gnaeus Scipio: Other writers, excepting Seneca, speak of but one daughter, and represent the dowry as given when Scipio was warring in Spain, in 218-211 B.C. Cf. Val. Max. IV.IV.10; Sen. Qu. Nat. I.XVII.9; Apul. Apol. 18; Ammian. Marc. XIV.VI.11.

58 poverty and honesty of Aristides: 468 B.C. Cf. Nep. Aristid. 3; Plut. Aristid. 25.

59 Epaminondas' belongings: 362 B.C. Cf. Plut. Fab. Max. 27; Nep. Epam. 3.

60 not more than two couches: Frontinus has in mind a Roman lectus, or dining-couch, which accommodated three persons.

61 Hannibal's frugal habits: Cf. Livy XXI.4; Sil. Ital. XII.559-560.

62 Masinissa at 90: 148 B.C. Cf. Polyb. XXXVI.16; Cic. de Sen. x.34.

63 Manius Curius satisfied with equality: Cf. Val. Max. IV.III.5; Plin. H. N. XVIII.4; Plut. Apophth. M'. Curii. Nep. Thras. 4 attributes a somewhat similar reply to Pittacus.

64 Scaurus' record: For the Memoirs of Scaurus, consul 115 B.C., cf. Val. Max. IV.IV.11; Tac. Agric. 1.

65 unharmed civilians will be grateful: 70 A.D. Cf. Introduction, p. xx.

66 Mummius' scrupulous honesty and sobriety: 146 B.C. Cf. Cic. de Off. II.XXII.76; in Verr. I.XXI.55; Plin. H. N. XXXIV.VII.17.

67 The schoolteacher of the Falisci: 394 B.C. Cf. Val. Max. VI.V.1; Livy V.27; Plut. Camil. 10; Polyaen. VIII.7.

68 Pyrrhus' corrupt doctor: 279 B.C. Cf. Livy Per. 13; Cic. de Off. III.XXII.86; Plut. Pyrrh. 21. Val. Max. VI.V.1 and Gell. III.8 represent Fabricius as disclosing the plot, but not the name of the traitor.

69 Pompey throws the fasces in the faces of his soldiers: 79 B.C. Cf. Plut. Pomp. 14, Apophth. Pomp. 5; Zonar. X.2. There is no mention of Glaucia in this connection elsewhere.

70 Caesar's firmness wins him respect: 49 B.C. Cf. Suet. Caes. 69; Appian B.C. II.47; Dio XLI.26 ff.

71 their leader: Viridomarius, the Insubrian Gaul.

72 spolia opima: Spoils taken from a victorious commander from the leader of the enemy.

73 Claudius Marcellus breaks thru: 222 B.C. Cf. Val. Max. III.II.5; Livy Per. 20; Plut. Marc. 6 ff.; Flor. II.4.

74 Lucius Paulus does not flee: 216 B.C. Cf. Livy XXII.49.

75 Varro lives with his defeat: Cf. Livy XXII.LXI.14-15; Val. Max. III.IV.4, IV.V.2.

76 smaller camp: When the Romans reached Cannae, they pitched two camps, the larger one on the N.W. bank of the Aufidus, the smaller on the S.E. bank, •about a mile and a quarter apart, according to Polyb. III.CX.10. Before the battle, Hannibal transferred his camp from the east side of the river to the west.

77 Tuditanus and Octavius break thru the lines: 216 B.C. Cf. Livy XXII.50; Appian Hann. 16. Livy gives the number of those escaping from the smaller camp as six hundred. Appian says ten thousand from the larger camp escaped. One leader only is mentioned by both.

78 Decius' diversion: Cf. I.V.14 and note.

79 Calpurnius Flamma's diversion: Cf. I.V.15 and note.

80 Caesar chooses the tenth legion: Cf. I.XI.3 and note.

81 Spartan attitude: Cf. Cic. Tusc. V.XIV.42; Val. Max. VI.IV.ext.4; Plut. Apophth. Lacon. Ignot. 50.°

82 Leonidas finds shade: Cf. Cic. Tusc. I.XLII.101; Val. Max. III.VII.ext.8.

83 Aelius' woodpecker: Cf. Plin. H. N. X.XVIII.20. Val. Max. V.VI.4 says that the Aelian family lost seventeen members at the battle of Cannae. The last sentence of this paragraph is undoubtedly an interpolation.

84 Publius Decius father and son: 340 & 295 B.C. Cf. Val. Max. V.VI.5, 6; Cic. de Fin. II.XIX.61, and frequently; Livy VIII.9, X.28.

85 Crassus escapes the disgrace of servitude: 130 B.C. Crassus was proconsul at the time of his death. Cf. Val. Max. III.II.12; Flor. II.XX.4-5; Oros. V.x.1-4.

86 Marcus Cato's sword: 168 B.C. Battle of Pydna. Cf. Val. Max. III.II.16; Justin. XXXIII.2. Plut. Aemil. 21 gives a slightly different story.

87 the resolve of the inhabitants of Petelia: 216 B.C. Cf. Livy XXIII.20, 30; Val. Max. VI.VI.ext.2; Appian Hann. 29.

88 the resolve of the inhabitants of Consabra: 79-75 B.C.

89 two hundred denarii: about £6 15s.

90 the mouse of Casilinum: 216 B.C. Cf. Val. Max. VII.VI.2, 3; Plin. H. N. VIII.LVII.82 Livy XXIII.19.

91 the resolve of the Cyzicenes: 74 B.C. Cf. Appian Mith. 73.

92 the resolve of the Segovians: 147-139 B.C.

93 the resolve of the Numantians: 133 B.C. Cf. Livy Per. 59; Val. Max. III.II.ext.7, VII.VI.ext.2; Sen. de Ira i.11.

94 Quintus Fabius: Quintus Fabius Maximus Cunctator. Cf. Sil. Ital. VII.539 ff. Plut. Apophth. Caec. Metell. relates a similar reply of Metellus.

95 Xenophon on foot: 401 B.C. Cf. Xen. Anab. III.IV.44-49.

96 Alexander's seat: Cf. Val. Max. V.I.ext.1; Curt. VIII.IV.15-17.

97 Caesar starves a cold: Cf. Veget. III.26; Appian Hisp. 87.

98 Lucius Paulus on thinking old: Cf. Livy XLIV.36; Gell. XIII.III.6; Plut. Apophth. Aemil. 5.

99 Sertorius' horsetails: Cf. I.X.1 and note.

100 Laevinus gives a spy the grand tour: 280 B.C. Cf. Eutrop. II.11; Zonar. VIII.3. Livy XXX.29, Appian Pun. 39 and Polyaen. VIII.XVI.8 attributes° a similar stratagem to Scipio.

101 the Varian disaster: The defeat of Varus by Arminius in the Teutoburg Forest in 9 A.D.

102 Caedicius' wood: Cf. Vell. II.120.

103 Hannibal's jars of vipers: Justin. XXXII.4 and Nep. Hann. 10 represent Hannibal as suggesting this device to Prusias.

104 Prusias' jars of vipers: 48 B.C. Cf. Caes. B.C. III.101.

105 Marcus Livius leaves a few enemies alive: 207 B.C. Cf. Livy XXVII.49. The Parthians did the same to the Romans in 54 B.C., Plut. Crassus, 28,

106 Scipio Africanus' paved road: Cf. Veget. III.21.

107 Paches' steel: Thuc. III.34 and Polyaen. III.2 cite another instance of the cunning treachery of Paches in 427 B.C.

108 Alcetas' single galley: 377 B.C. Cf. Polyaen. II.7. Caes. B.C. III.24 relates a similar stratagem employed by Antony.

109 Ptolemy's dust-raising animals: 321 B.C. Cf. Polyaen. IV.19. Front. II.IV.1 relates a somewhat similar device of Papirius Cursor.

110 Myronides states the odds: 457 B.C. Cf. Polyaen. I.XXXV.2.

111 Gaius Pinarius corrals the enemy: 214 B.C. Cf. Livy XXIV.37-39; Polyaen. VIII.21.

112 They welcomed Iphicrates, unfortunately: 390-389 B.C. Cf. Polyaen. III.IX.58.

113 Tiberius Gracchus' volunteer slaves: 214 B.C. Cf. Livy XXIV.14-16.

114 the "Latin Name": i.e. the Latin League. The cities of Latium were from very early times united in an alliance with Rome. At first this bond was of a political nature, on a basis of perfect equality; later Rome became the leading power and assumed the supremacy.

115 Hannibal divides the Latin League: 217 B.C. Cf. Livy XXII.6, 7, 13; Polyb. III.77, 84-85.

116 Mago's phantom reinforcements: 208 B.C. Cf. Livy XXVII.28.

117 Scipio Aemilianus attaches archers and slingers to all his units: 133 B.C. Veget. I.15 narrates instances of the important part played in Roman battles by archers and javelin throwers, and emphasizes the necessity of training in archery.

118 Pelopidas burns his bridge: 369-364 B.C.

119 Naevius' short feisty guys: 211 B.C. Cf. Livy XXVI.4; Val. Max. II.III.3.

120 Publius Scipio seizes on a demoralized enemy: 190 B.C. Cf. Livy XXXVII.37, 39; Flor. II.VIII.17.

121 Cato's phantom reinforcements: 195 B.C. Cf. Livy XXXIV.11-13.

122 Caesar aims at the faces and eyes of the enemy: 48 B.C. Cf. Plut. Caes. 44-45, Pomp. 69; Polyaen. VIII.XXIII.25.

123 the Voccaei dress up: 179-178 B.C.

124 Eumenes of Cardia devises stationary exercise machines for his horses: 320 B.C. Cf. Nep. Eumen. 5; Plut. Eumen. 11; Diodor. XVIII.42.

125 Cato promises money: 195 B.C. Cf. Plut. Cat. Maj. 10.

126 Quintus Maximus insures loyalty: Cf. III.XVI.1 and note; Plut. Fab. 20.

127 Philip: The father of Alexander.

128 Titius Quinctius Crispinus sends out an alert against Hannibal's counterfeit letters: 208 B.C. Cf. Livy XXVII.28.

129 Publius Scipio makes the Romans stand their ground: 216 B.C. Cf. Livy XXII.53; Val. Max. V.VI.7; Sil. Ital. X.426 ff.

130 Camillus burns down the enemy camp: 389 B.C. Cf. Livy VI.II.9-11; Plut. Cam. 34.

131 Crassus' camp burned down: 90 B.C.

132 Quintus Metellus' virtual ambush turns out real: 143-142 B.C.

Made in United States
Troutdale, OR
11/10/2023

14467224R00056